Abused

Abused

Surviving Sexual Assault and a
Toxic Gymnastics Culture

Rachel Haines

ROWMAN & LITTLEFIELD
Lanham • Boulder • New York • London

Published by Rowman & Littlefield
An imprint of The Rowman & Littlefield Publishing Group, Inc.
4501 Forbes Boulevard, Suite 200, Lanham, Maryland 20706
www.rowman.com

6 Tinworth Street, London SE11 5AL

Distributed by NATIONAL BOOK NETWORK

British Library Cataloguing in Publication Information Available

Library of Congress Cataloging-in-Publication Data
Names: Haines, Rachel (Gymnast), author.
Title: Abused : surviving sexual assault and a toxic gymnastics culture / Rachel
   Haines.
Description: Lanham, Maryland : Rowman & Littlefield, [2019] | Includes
   bibliographical references and index.
Identifiers: LCCN 2018041560 (print) | LCCN 2019001066 (ebook) | ISBN
   9781538123867 (electronic) | ISBN 9781538123850 (cloth : alk. paper)
Subjects: LCSH: Haines, Rachel. | Gymnasts—United States—Biography. |
   Women gymnasts—United States—Biography. | Rape victims—United States—
   Biography. | Sexual abuse victims—United States—Biography. | Gymnastics—
   Social aspects—United States. | Gymnastics—Corrupt practices—United States. |
   Gymnastics—Moral and ethical aspects—United States.
Classification: LCC GV460.2.H35 (ebook) | LCC GV460.2.H35 A3 2019 (print) |
   DDC 796.44092 [B] —dc23
LC record available at https://lccn.loc.gov/2018041560

∞™ The paper used in this publication meets the minimum requirements of
American National Standard for Information Sciences—Permanence of Paper
for Printed Library Materials, ANSI/NISO Z39.48-1992.

Printed in the United States of America

Contents

	Readers Note	vii
	Letter to My Future Daughter	ix
	Prologue	xi
Chapter 1	The Beginning	1
Chapter 2	Gedderts' Twistars USA	9
Chapter 3	Larry	17
Chapter 4	Broken	21
Chapter 5	Diagnosis	29
Chapter 6	Unworthy	37
Chapter 7	Medicated	43
Chapter 8	All on the Floor	51
Chapter 9	College	63
Chapter 10	Divided	69
Chapter 11	Last One, Best One	75
Chapter 12	NCAAs	85

Chapter 13   Retirement   91

Chapter 14   Numb   95

Chapter 15   Healing, Preparing, Recovery   101

Chapter 16   The Trial   113

Chapter 17   Still, I Rise   121

              Epilogue   123

              About the Author   127

Readers Note

Reader discretion is advised. My story contains vulnerable, personal, and explicit descriptions of my experiences as a gymnast. This includes multiple illustrations and depictions of my interactions with US gymnastics team doctor and convicted serial child molester Larry Nassar and Olympic US gymnastics coach John Geddert.

A plea: Please do not assume my experiences were the same as *anyone* else's accounts. Though there are hundreds of other survivors, my story is *only* mine, and I did not write this book to explain the accounts of others.

As a survivor, I wholeheartedly believe everyone has a voice that deserves to be heard. Everyone's experiences matter equally and should be equally trusted and believed.

This story is mine, and mine alone. I am Survivor 195.

~

Letter to My Future Daughter

Dear Daughter,

I know one day you'll hold this book in your small, sweet hands. You'll read these words I've painfully strung together, and you'll know how I feel about you doing gymnastics. You'll read what I went through, and you'll know every detail, and it will hurt. You'll understand my fear of the gymnastics culture and my passionate desire to protect you from what I experienced. You'll read clear and haunting descriptions of what your mom went through, and I will hate it. I will hate having you imagine what my experiences were, and I will dread the fire in you that wants to be a gymnast yourself.

But don't let it stop you.

I will always fuel the fire that burns in your heart to do what you love. I will never push you to do anything, and I will not stop you from try-ing anything and everything that you want to try. If gymnastics ends up on that list, it's okay. I will bring you to every practice and sit at every meet, embracing every second I get to watch you do what you love. I will feel joy watching your passion radiate through your sport. I promise to always and forever be your number one fan no matter what your heart leads you to do. Actress, bookworm, painter, musician, or gymnast, I promise I will be your loudest cheerleader. In the crowd. On the sidelines. Next to you.

I also promise to protect you with everything I have and every inch of my being. I will guard you with every ounce of strength in me from what I know the sport could do to you. I will build you up, I will pay attention, I will support you, I will listen. I will watch for warning signs, and I will fight for you. Just like my parents were for me, I will be your guardian.

Gymnast or not, I promise to help you become the strong and independent woman I know you can and will be.

~

Prologue

I am getting to the stage in my life where people frequently ask, "Will you let your daughter do gymnastics?" And I have a hard time answering. I struggle to imagine my little girl being thrown into the sport that, at points, tore me to pieces. I flash back to those dreadful days in the gym that brought me so much fear and anxiety. I remember those experiences with skills, coaches, meets, and trainers that still appear in my nightmares today. Each time I cautiously answer that question with, "She can do gymnastics if she chooses to do so." But if I were completely honest, my answer would be, "I will never *put* my daughter in gymnastics."

From the outside in, the sport looks to be the optimal choice for athletic development. At a young age, it teaches you balance, body awareness, how to safely fall, and coordination. As you progress and grow through the sport, it teaches you perseverance, coachability, and courage. It strengthens you physically, mentally, and emotionally. Young children always appear to be at the peak of happiness as they jump into the foam pits, bounce off of the football field–sized trampolines, and swing from the ropes. It looks fun, teaches valuable life skills, and builds character. It checks all the boxes.

Which is every parent's dream, right?

Only those who endure gymnastics through their childhood and teenage years see the sport's true colors. As you're growing and developing, if you chose gymnastics, you are signing yourself up to be completely dedicated and focused on the sport, especially if you intend to be a college athlete or an Olympian. Your life revolves around gymnastics. No football games, no school dances, no sleepovers at your friends' houses. The way you live, eat, and sleep is dependent on the demands of your practices. How can you be out late at a friend's house on Friday night when you have a five-hour workout at 8:00 a.m. the next day?

The answer is: You can't.

Not only is gymnastics physically demanding, it also changes your mental development. I did not recognize the full effect gymnastics had on me until I was more than a year retired from it. I learned how being constantly compared to perfection had a toll on my confidence. My life revolved around striving for that perfect 10.0, and now my lifestyle outside of the sport reaches for it too. I saw how living in a leotard created an unhealthy expectation for my body image. I started comparing myself at a young age to other gymnasts, thinking their bodies looked better in leotards than mine did, and thinking that some gymnasts scored higher because they were skinnier. As a middle schooler, I was only wearing leotards that made me feel small, ones that were just a little baggy and dark colored. I was also trained to think that power and authority trumped comfort and morals. I was surrounded by figures who used intimidation as a method of control, figures who would use that intimidation to abuse me.

My path through gymnastics was, at times, very rough. I experienced major transitions, serious injury, sexual abuse, loss of coaches, and early retirement due to injury. I competed at the highest level in high school, was on the national team for two years, and competed for a top-ranked Division I school. I can see how gymnastics taught me hundreds of skills and life lessons and gave me unlimited, amazing opportunities. I reaped the benefits of being a Division I athlete and continue to receive perks from having developed the physical and mental skills that gymnastics taught me. I have traveled to different countries and performed in almost all fifty states simply because I was a competitive gymnast. But I have also seen the dark side of the sport that consumed my childhood. I've personally experienced the poisonous culture that accompanies the sport so many dream their children will excel at—a culture that's *long* overdue for change.

I will not be one of those parents who controls my child in an unhealthy way. When I say that I will not sign her up for gymnastics, I mean I will not be the one who introduces her to the sport. I cannot protect her from hearing the kids brag at school at how they jumped into the foam pits and I cannot stop her curiosity from wanting to do it too. The day she comes to me and says, "Momma, I want to do flips just like you did!" I will stare into the same big brown eyes my parents did and say, "Okay."

CHAPTER ONE

~

The Beginning

I will be the first to admit my life has been handed to me on a silver platter because I was a gymnast. I have bachelor's and master's degrees paid for by the University of Minnesota, which many people would say is enough to make gymnastics alone worth doing. The outrageous amount of loans most young adults my age face is horrendous, and I know how lucky I am to be completely debt free with "MA" after my name. I have endless coaching job opportunities because of my extensive years of experience. My résumé is crammed full of references, desired skills, and accolades, just because of gymnastics. There were undoubtedly rewards to being the caliber of athlete that I was, rewards that I am entirely thankful for.

But in recent months, I've found myself reflecting on what I was put through. I had the most supportive and protective parents as my guardians, and they still could not protect me from the horrors that come with the sport. Knowing that I had the best people possible behind me and they still weren't enough to keep me safe has solidified my refusal to ever sign my children up for gymnastics. No matter the scholarship amounts my children may get through the sport, there is no price that could ever repay me for the experiences that I went through as a gymnast.

Some days, I wish I had debt instead.

Writing my story gave me the opportunity to reflect on my many years as a gymnast and to pay attention to where things started to turn sour. I focused in on the small hints, the foreshadowing of the horrors that would come. It is obviously easier to reflect on the more recent memories, but pulling out details from my early days as a gymnast started to fuel the lightbulb of realization about how something so terrible could come from a sport that I had loved so much.

I truly feel God wanted and designed me to be a gymnast. I know it was my calling, and my parents could see it, too. Before I could walk or stand on my own, I was hanging on the fridge handle begging for my bottle. I was flipping off the end of the couch onto stacks of pillows, always looking for new ways to tumble and toss my body.

My parents frequently share stories about how I would even find new ways to ride playground slides. One time I found a creative entrance that resulted in me hanging from the top of the slide with just my little hands gripping onto the side of it. I lost my grip, and my parents ran to catch me before I hit the ground, but I fell too quickly. I fell, bouncing off my bum onto the hard ground. I looked up at them as if nothing had happened.

I was always driven to learn new skills and apparently was okay with falling while learning them. It seemed extremely fitting to get me into a gymnastics class.

Gymnastics starts out as bubbly and inviting as it gets: Mommy and Me classes filled with young children given an hour to jump on trampolines and throw foam blocks around. It was incredible bonding time with my mom, great training for my body, and an excellent outlet for my unlimited energy. I see pictures of myself at three years old, loving the time I spent in the gym. I was obsessed with the feeling of flipping. I have vague memories of my time at my first gym. Initially, I was in the waiting room portion of it while my sister was in her classes. I remember the big windows I looked through to watch her. I remember playing with LEGOs to keep myself busy while every ounce of me wanted to be down there with her. I remember my first classes. The feeling of being strapped into a belt where coaches lifted me sky high into the air above trampolines. Jumping off what felt like mountains of mats into the foam pits. Sprinting down the tumble track at full speed just to go flying into the pit at the end. I fell in love with the feeling of flying, and, in turn, with gymnastics.

Another story my mom shares involves the time she was approached by coaches after the Mommy and Me classes concluded. My coaches confirmed that my love for the sport was accompanied by a natural talent for it, and they suggested I should continue the sport at the next level.

My parents never forced me to do anything. Even at four years old, they asked me what I wanted to do and made sure I knew I was supported regardless of the decision I made. My love for the sport was immeasurable, and I chose to continue. I moved up to training with the team that put on shows at the end of every year. I got my first choreographed routine, and even though it was with the twenty other girls in my class, I felt like the Olympians I saw on TV. I performed my cartwheels and roundoffs like they were my passes at the Olympics.

I started to see the perks of being a gymnast in elementary school. I excelled at every physical test. I am still the record holder for push-ups, sit-ups, and flexibility in my elementary school almost fifteen years later. My name remains on a board hung above the gym for all to see. I loved being the best, and I was driven to be the strongest. I even made it a priority to be better than the strongest male in our school. Neither age nor gender was going to scare me away from trying to be better than everyone. At six years old, my competitiveness made me a force to be reckoned with. I was almost untouchable.

I remember how excited I would be when one of my friends hosted a birthday party at a gym. It meant I got to show off every new trick I had learned in my gymnastics classes. I was proud to be a little gymnast and used every opportunity to perform for others and impress them. Starting in first grade, I participated in the elementary school talent show, exhibiting all the skills I ever learned. I was fearless. My performance became an annual tradition, and every year talk spread like wildfire before the show about the skills I was going to perform for my school that year.

"This year she's doing a backflip!!"

"I heard she's doing two in a row!!"

Year after year, my performance in the show was saved for last, as it was the most anticipated, and I loved it. I sat behind the curtain while everyone else performed, feeling the adrenaline surge through my body as one after another's talent finished. I heard the excited mumbles in the crowd as the mats were laid out before my turn. I fed off of the anticipation for me every year from first to fourth grade.

In fifth grade, my final year in elementary school, I initially wanted to do something different for the talent show. Instead of my usual upgraded routine, I wanted to dedicate a song to my sister. I wanted to sing her "Wind beneath My Wings." I practiced singing it every car ride to practice. I learned all of the lyrics and was ready to perform for her. But as the show approached, my school learned I wasn't doing gymnastics and made their disappointment clear. I felt my anxiety as their expectations for my performance matched those they had for my gymnastics—but for my singing instead.

I was not a singer; I was a gymnast. I let my fear of failing keep me from trying something new. I stayed in my comfort zone and performed what I knew I wouldn't fail at. I showed them my gymnastics routine one last time.

I fed off the popularity my sport graced me with. I thrived off the excitement it contagiously gave my peers. Even at eight years old, the doors were wide open for gymnastics to become my identity. I was letting myself be known as "the gymnast." This identity would stick with me until the day I hung up the leotard one last time. Everyone knew I spent hours training at the gym, that I knew how to do skills no human should be able to do, and that I had the dream of being one of the best gymnasts in the world. They all knew I was rapidly reaching the transition from fun acrobatics classes to competitive gymnastics.

I started at a very small gym that specialized in preschool classes. Shortly after, I moved to a gym that focused most of its attention on younger children's skills. I switched gyms again around age seven to a competitive gym. I vividly remember the day I tried out for my new gym. The owner of the gym, who was also the head coach, led me around to all of the events, asking me to show off all of the skills that I knew. I typically loved this type of spotlight, but this time was different. I felt a spur of nerves and anxiety. In each and every talent show in the past, I had felt pure excitement and adrenaline. This was the first time I was worried about my performance quality. It always had impressed everyone because I could do things that they could not, but this coach taught the best of the best at the highest level. She had not only seen everything, she had done it herself years ago. I knew my recreational level skills were unimpressive to her.

I showed her everything. At one point she brought me to the bars and asked if I could jump to the highbar. I had never done it before, but I made myself do it for her. Her authority in the gym made me want to do everything in my power to impress her—even if it meant doing something I was not comfortable with. At seven years old, I knew what I did for her impacted where I would be placed in the gym, who I would get to train with, and what level I would get to compete at. One person controlled how far ahead I could jump from everyone else. One person could put me on the path to being the best.

This marks the very first sign of a flawed sport culture.

But my coach at this new gym was remarkable. She is the person who made my talent for a hobby into a passion for a sport. She put herself into her gymnasts' shoes as much as she could to understand us as people instead of just competitors. She was a part of everything we did as a team, which made our bonding experiences much more valuable. She was at every pool party and team gathering, and she even participated in our annual spirit weeks.

Seeing her throw on black leotards at fifty years old to match her team on Goth Day is a memory I will never forget.

I quickly moved through competitive levels 3–7, skipping a few in between. For those who aren't well versed in the sport, the transition to level 7 is a larger jump than the transitions between the previous levels. It has harder requirements to meet, greater difficulty in skills, and is the first year you are out of the compulsory stage. The only difference nongymnasts see about level 7 is that it is the level where the same routine and same floor music are no longer performed one million times at competitions. In level 7, we got to choose our own music, make up our choreography, and pick the skills we wanted to perform to meet the level's requirements.

My first floor routine was choreographed to be bubbly, sassy, and cute. Most gymnasts' routines are. It was a lot of shimmying and shaking that made audiences and judges smile while I performed it. My coach always told me the more I shook, shimmied, and smiled, the more "cutesy points" I got from the judges. Although she said it to motivate me to show off my routine more, I truly believe "cutesy points" existed.

I was blessed to not experience any serious and long-term injuries while I was at this gym. I broke my tailbone and sternum, but both meant just a few weeks off and icing regularly. My coach handled our injuries very well. She trusted us and made it clear that we only got out of our training what we put into it. If we wanted to sit out for aches and pains, our scores at competitions would reflect it.

I didn't need any motivation to come back from injuries. My competitiveness hated sitting out on more opportunities to win.

I had a close group of friends as my teammates. I have honestly always had great friends as a result of the sport, but teammates here were something kids my age did not typically have. We did not have cliques, and we argued like sisters. When you spend forty hours a week together, you are basically family.

Our level 8 team was phenomenal. We were one of the strongest teams in the state. We knocked off the usual team title winners and were a threat to any gym we went up against. My teammates and I were consistent and strong. We thrived off of each other, and there was a healthy competition between us for the top scores of the meet. I *loved* competing with my team. There was no pressure, no fear, no worry of failure. We had so much fun competing.

This time of my life was when my love for the sport was pure and my relationship with it was healthy. Like with any sport, I would come home from practices crying some days if I had fallen a lot or twisted an ankle. My mom always used to say, "Do you want to go to practice tomorrow? Or do you want to be done?" She never made me feel like I had to continue or that she was pressuring me to get to the highest level. My parents were amazing and reminded me that the second I stopped loving the sport, there was nothing stopping me from quitting and finding a new passion.

If my daughter decides she wants to do gymnastics herself, I hope I am able to mirror the way my parents made me feel in instances like this.

Even though I clearly loved and thrived in gymnastics, my parents wanted me to try everything to make sure I wasn't just settling for the only sport I knew. They signed me up for soccer, dance, and piano lessons. I watched as my frustration at my lack of talent in other things only drove me to push myself harder in gymnastics. Nothing came as easily as gymnastics, and I resented it. Shortly after realizing I wasn't good at soccer, I showed everyone my gymnastics skills on the field instead. Back handspring, back handspring, back handspring. Here I was trying to prove my athleticism to seven-year-olds because I knew they saw me as weak in soccer. My thirst for attention was cringeworthy. Why wasn't I okay with not being the best at something?

Why am I still not okay with not being the best at everything?

Like every sport, there were rewards for being the best. When I was young, it was ribbons. If you performed well, you got a blue ribbon; if you performed decently, a red ribbon; if you failed, a rainbow ribbon. After meets, teams stood together displaying all of their earned ribbons for pictures. If I didn't have four blue ribbons, displaying my awards for a picture mortified me. I felt embarrassed. I hadn't done my best, and that feeling was worse than not being the best. Later in my career, the award for being the best became medals. If I didn't have the most medals around my neck, I didn't want to be in any team pictures, either.

I see now that when I was young I had a fear of failing. I was terrified at people seeing me not meet my full potential. It started when I was young and continues to haunt me now. It began at my tryouts with my new gym. I was scared my performance failed to meet the coach's expectations. It continued when I gave up singing my sister a song at the talent show. I knew I was going to fail compared to what I could do in gymnastics. It turned from fear and embarrassment as a child to stress and anxiety as an adult.

It changed from fear of failing in my sport into fear of failing in all aspects of my life.

I so wish that I had committed to playing another sport when I was this young. I wish that I had not given up trying new things, like when I wasn't good at soccer. Now, at twenty-three, I have picked up golf and tennis, but first had to push past my anger with myself when I didn't learn it as easily as I learned gymnastics. I am so happy that I have people in my life who make me work through my impatience. The number of times I have wanted to pick up a golf ball and drop it farther ahead toward the green is too high to count. My fiancé knows how to get under my skin when I lean down to grab my ball. He always says, "You won't get better if you keep picking it up, Rach." Or, "No, hit it again. We're not in a rush, just try one more time."

I sympathize with those who have to teach me new things because of my impatience during the climb to perfection or satisfaction with my performance. It has to be similar to teaching a child. If I had learned that sometimes skills aren't developed just through talent back then, maybe I would be a better golf partner today.

CHAPTER TWO

~

Gedderts' Twistars USA

My team that had dominated the level 7 and 8 competitions progressed together, and we all moved up to level 9 the same year. We were again a large threat to even the best gyms in the nation.

In seventh grade, I competed in my first Regional Competition. The structure of gymnastics is unique compared to every other sport. Our State Meet is at the least competitive end of our competitions, and doing well at State qualifies you to Regionals. Doing well at Regionals gets you a ticket to Nationals, the most competitive meet in club gymnastics.

In 2008 I walked into my first Regional Competition wide-eyed and filled to the eyeballs with excitement. I watched the session before mine and observed the girls who had earned their spot at Nationals. I analyzed what they had to do to get to the next level of competition. I saw them look so thrilled to get fitted for their National leotards. I wanted to represent my region in the beautiful leos, too.

I told myself to put everything I had into my performances, and I poured my heart into my routines. I started on floor, my favorite event. I no longer had the shimmying and shaking routine, but I still was showing my choreography off to the best of my ability. I was still trying to earn myself "cutesy points," just in case they did exist. Starting on floor gave me the confidence to propel myself through the meet. Vault was easy for me in level 9. It was all power and no technique, but somehow I made it around. Bars was my weakest event . . . always was.

Watching old videos, it looks extremely out of control, but somehow I always made it. I ended my competition on beam and stuck my last routine's dismount. My coach stalked the updating scores and kept track of my place throughout the competition. Top 8 qualified for Nationals, and she knew what I needed on the last event to qualify.

She knew after my last routine that I had made it.

I stood on that podium beaming with happiness. I was going to get to go to Missouri and compete at the most prestigious competition in club gymnastics. Again, I was so proud to be a gymnast. My pride continued as training for Nationals in 2007 was unbelievably fun. After qualifying to the hardest competition to get into, there is nothing to stress about achieving. I didn't have my heart set on being a National Champion; I was just ecstatic to be going at all. I was embracing every moment.

My mom and aunt drove me down to Missouri themselves to support me at my first Nationals. On the drive down, I suffered a migraine. This had become a regular occurrence, and I was getting them more and more often. We had been trying to figure out what caused them for more than a year. I knew I was getting one when I started seeing "the spots." One of my eyes would always go completely blind over the period of a half hour, and once I could see again I was hit with the most debilitating headache you can imagine. I wanted to gouge my eyes out whenever one came on. It felt like my eyes were falling out; that's how bad it hurt. I was getting migraines more frequently, and they were becoming something that would stop me from functioning for many hours. They would not subside enough for me to function again until I had thrown up, taken medication, and slept for at least three hours. I laid in the backseat, head pounding and feeling moments away from throwing up, and tried to start to sleep it off.

We got to the hotel and I went straight to bed. I was so excited to practice the next day in the arena that I couldn't fall asleep, but my migraine needed me to. I maybe got two hours of sleep. I woke up exhausted and my head was sore. We went to the arena and I got to see where I would be competing the following day. I got to touch the equipment and see who I was competing against for the first time. After watching a few other gymnasts, I was no longer excited to compete—I was terrified.

These girls were flawless. Their difficulty was much greater than mine, and their routines were undeniably more impressive. I said to my mom, "Everyone has a double back on floor. I have never even tried a double back on floor." I remember in significant detail how sick I felt at how unqualified I was. I did not deserve to be there. My floor routine was nowhere near as impressive as everyone else's. My gymnastics dropped below my own expectations.

I hated my skills. I doubted my talent. I went home after practice ashamed of the gymnast that I was. I wish I didn't have a cookie-cutter routine. I was embarrassed and upset. I was so easily affected by how I felt about gymnastics because it had evolved into my entire identity.

The morning of the competition was normal. I woke up and got ready. My mom put my hair in a tight bun with three thousand bobby pins piercing my skull like usual. I ate my lucky ice cream sandwich for breakfast, like I always did before meets, and headed to the arena. I walked in and already felt belittled. I was comparing myself to every single gymnast there. I lost all self-confidence, as the one talent I had was nothing to be proud of here.

I was losing my identity.

I started on beam. I was warming up when they started. The spots. Anxiety took over my little body as I realized both that I was about to be in excruciating pain and that my meet was over. They began flooding further over my eye and I could feel myself trying to fight it. As the blindness took over I no longer felt safe doing my routine on a four-inch beam. I found my mom in the crowd, and I signed, "I have the spots."

I could see her heart shatter for me. She knew, too, that I wasn't going to be able to finish the meet. My first Nationals was over. I would have to wait a full year for another opportunity to compete at this meet, and again I would have to earn my spot.

On the drive back to Michigan right after we left the arena, we had to pull the car over multiple times so I could throw up from my excruciating headache. I tried to sleep it off so that I wasn't in so much pain, but I was experiencing a combination of car sickness along with my migraine. The drive home was terrible. I was physically and emotionally broken. Going home without even getting to compete at my first Nationals was heartbreaking. I was going to do everything in my power to make sure I didn't feel this way again next year.

I am so happy to say that I have grown out of my migraines. They stopped occurring once I had my braces removed. Was there an association? I am not sure. But I am so thankful that I have not experienced one of these excruciating moments in more than seven years.

I worked harder than ever to get a chance to get back to Nationals again in 2008. I was pushing myself to get my identity back. I added a double back to my floor routine. I actually upgraded everything. I made sure that if I was going back to this meet, I was going back with confidence in my abilities. The season flew by, and Regionals arrived. Again, I poured my heart into my routines. I left everything I had on the floor. I was more confident in my gymnastics just because I had some of the skills that I had been intimidated by the year before. I approached each event with a different kind of belief in myself, and it showed. I nailed every event and became more and more energized as the meet progressed. I was giving my all to every performance. I was showing my passion through my routines. I built back up my identity through success in my sport and it made me happy again. I was having fun again. I was doing my gymnastics for me and for me alone.

And I won.

My coach came over to me after the meet had concluded. I had my Maui Wowie drink in hand, and she had told me where I had finished. I was the Regional Champion. I stood on top of the podium with such pride. I was just as excited about qualifying the second time as I was the first. I was not going to waste my hard work again. I was more than motivated to get back in the gym and train for Nationals. I was honored to receive the beautiful leo I would wear for my next Nationals.

Then, unexpectedly in eighth grade, I went through my first emotional distress with gymnastics.

It was a normal day; all of my teammates and I stood huddled near our lockers before practice started. We were training for our second Nationals, so practices were fun and lighthearted. But then our coach came to us with none of her usual peppy enthusiasm and said she had news.

She explained that our gym had been sold and purchased by a new owner who wanted to clear out the coaching staff and start over. In other words, our coach was leaving. I know this had a traumatic effect on me because of how vividly I remember that day. Our team was in chaos. Moms snatched their daughters moments after the news broke and stated, "We're going to try out other gyms right now and see what is a good fit. We will keep you posted on what we find."

In their defense, quick action was needed. This change had oc-
curred two weeks before Nationals. We needed gyms to train at, and
we needed our coach—who had gotten us this far—to continue coaching us. There was a clear panic that overtook our gym, and I felt a buzz
of emotions that I couldn't handle. I believe at this moment, I had my
very first anxiety attack.

I had no idea where I was going to go.

Did I want to go to a different gym?

*If you know me personally, you know last-minute plan changes give me
severe anxiety. Part of me wonders if it was partially because of this event.
Now, everything in my life follows a strict and structured plan. Deviation
from that plan causes my chest to turn red, my mind to race, and my body
to tremble. I hate this quality about myself, and I hate my dependence on
schedules accompanied by my inflexibility when they change.*

My coach connected with numerous gyms in the hopes of finding one
that would let her team train there until Nationals. She called many
gyms that morning with the goal of finding one that could keep us
all together in one place. Only one coach responded with genuine
empathy and welcomed us along with our coach into his gym: Ged-
derts' Twistars.

Everyone knew this gym. It had the most accomplished and competitive reputation in the nation. It housed Elite Program competitors,
National Champions, and hopeful Olympians. Gymnasts feared the
blue leotards that were worn by Twistars gymnasts. Seeing them walk
into competitions meant accepting second place. John Geddert had
established himself as a successful coach and built up his reputation
to make himself a respected figure in the gymnastics world. Everyone
knew him. He walked with such power and leadership that it was terrifying to look at. There was no denying that he was the most intimidating figure in the gymnastics world.

He was known for his ruthless competitiveness and his ability to
breed perfection. He had given hundreds of young women the training to receive full-ride gymnastics scholarships to Division I colleges.
Everyone knew that if you trained at Twistars, you would be training
like a champion, and you would compete like a champion. This type
of training is not for everyone, and going to Twistars came with a huge
sacrifice. It was a cost everyone knew they would pay before they even

came. If you trained the way John wanted you to train, he would do his best to make sure you reaped the benefits of it. He would invite universities to the gym to recruit, he would contact college coaches to draw attention to his available gymnasts, and he would work hard to make sure his girls got the opportunity to compete at the collegiate level. If the training and coaching style didn't match your personality, you did not train at Twistars and John did not help you get a full-ride.

Here he was, inviting us into his gym, giving us full access to prepare for Nationals. He hired our coach so she would be able to coach us through the remainder of the season and still earn a living. He made me question my previously drawn negative conclusions about his personality. He was selflessly giving us his gym, knowing he would not get any credit for it at Nationals.

I remember my first practice at Twistars vividly. My team and I huddled together in a close circle before practice began as the Twistars girls huddled in their own cluster on the other side of the floor. We followed them through warm-ups, let them lead us through stretches, and followed the structure they did for practices. I was put on bars first. I wanted to do everything to stay out of the way of the Twistars team. After all, I was invading *their* gym. It seemed like every girl was training for Nationals there, and nobody was taking it lightly.

I guess that is the difference between a gym that makes qualifiers and a gym that breeds champions.

Switching gyms and equipment in gymnastics is a lot harder than you can imagine. For example, each beam is dramatically different. You get some that have sharp edges, some that are slippery, and some that feel two inches wide instead of four. Bars are all different, too. Some are wobbly, some are bouncy, and some are so tight they don't move the way we need them to in order to successfully perform our skills. Every gym that I have ever been to has a "good" set of bars that every girl prefers to use. Conversely, every gym has a "bad" set of bars everyone avoids. Being a brand-new member of the gym, I had no idea which set was which at Twistars.

But I learned quickly.

Nobody was using the red Spieth bars, and there were lines for the other sets. I wanted to impress John with my effort and willingness to take hundreds of turns since I was not going to impress him with my gymnastics. I volunteered myself to use the untouched Spieth bars.

Dumb.

These bars were the bounciest set I had ever used. They wobbled and shifted at every movement, and catching a release—let alone hitting a handstand—was near impossible for someone who had never used them before. I looked like a mess, and I felt even worse. I took thirty turns, all unsuccessful at completing even half of a routine. After falling for what felt like the thousandth time, I saw John watching.

I could feel my chest get flaming hot, my head spin, and my throat close up. I was not meeting my full potential and I was failing: my two biggest fears. I was failing in front of the person I wanted to impress the most. I hit my emotional breaking point and started to cry.

I remember thinking, "Great. Now he thinks I suck *and* I'm a baby."

I will never forget what John did next. He came over to me, softened his usual stern and cold voice, and said, "You don't like these bars much, do you?" I shook my head no, trying to make eye contact to show him respect, but my eyes were too watery to see his face clearly. He then said, "My girls hate these bars. I was very impressed you chose them. I have my Elites use them, as these are the bars that they use for international competitions."

John Geddert was showing me he understood my frustration?

He looked at me, pointed to the bars that had lines of gymnasts waiting to use them, and said, "I think you will like these two sets of bars better. I know it has been a difficult transition, but my gym is open to you. Don't let a set of Spieth bars be an unnecessary stress before Nationals."

I was comforted by John. To this day, I truly cannot understand why he had a soft spot for me. I was just an untalented crybaby for all he knew at this point. I think he could see my potential. Perhaps he knew my desire to outwork his team on my first day was out of respect for him.

I wanted to deserve to be there.

Nationals came even quicker than I had imagined. I traveled with the Twistars team but stayed with my coach. I was so relieved it was finally time to compete after the stressful and chaotic few weeks leading up to it. Again, I watched the girls who were warming up. I felt more confident this year about my abilities. I felt like I belonged at the competition, but I was nervous about impressing my new coaches. I felt like I was trying out again, with the added stress of it being the most competitive event of my season and for one of the most successful gyms in the nation.

My first event went solid. Again, it was beam. God was clearly giving me another chance to prove myself after the Nationals the year before. I stopped watching the competition and only cared about doing my personal best to impress my new coaches at Twistars. By the last rotation, I had no idea where I was in the rankings, but both my coaches had a different attitude about my last event.

I figured they were just excited about the competition almost being done.

It wasn't until I was almost up when the Twistars coach approached me and said, "Rachel, you can win." Goosebumps shot through my body in disbelief.

Me? A National Champion? Could two weeks at Twistars really do that to my gymnastics?

Of course my last event was bars, the event that made my first practice at the new gym so horrendous. Again, God was giving me an opportunity for redemption. He was letting me show my full potential. For some reason, I wasn't nervous. I faced the judge to salute and begin my routine and saw the gymnast who was in second place standing behind the judges table . . . watching. She was watching to see if I would fail, and she would become a National Champion instead. She was waiting for me to hand her the trophy because of an error.

She will never understand how much that motivated me.

The routine felt like it was in slow motion. For every movement I was concentrating hard, saying my cue words, and preparing for the skill that would follow.

"Handstand. Slow. Tight. Breathe. Squeeze. Release." I remember how slow my dismount felt. My ears drowned out all of the noise, and I felt my feet hit the ground.

Stuck.

At my second Nationals, I became a National Champion.

~

CHAPTER THREE

Larry

I was surprised at how much I meshed with these girls I had once seen as gymnastics robots. My respect for John continued to grow as I trained for him. I could tell he cared about me because of how much I respected him. I was one of the few gymnasts that he never yelled at. I truly think he coached every person individually. Some of his gymnasts needed a greater shove to be motivated, and others were more goal-oriented on their own. Those who disrespected him by rolling their eyes, cheating on assignments, and skipping practice were treated with equal disrespect from him. Relationships were two-way streets to John.

My first summer at Twistars was harder than anything I had ever done before. For one, Twistars was an hour and a half away from my home, so 8:00 a.m. practices meant getting up at 5:45 every morning. We trained just the same as we did in season, never stopping to rest and always looking for ways to perfect the smallest deductions. I learned quickly why they were the cleanest, most consistent, and most competitive team in the nation.

Summers at Twistars also meant running. Oh, how I hated the running. John would gather the entire morning practice team and have us move outside. We did a sprinting sequence: sprint for thirty seconds, rest for ten seconds. This mirrored the endurance requirements for a floor routine.

I remember thinking, "No wonder Twistars gymnasts can make it through such difficult routines; they're trained for a marathon-length floor routine." We ran every day. On days where John could tell we were tired and hurting, he would let us stretch instead. There were always girls who would try to make up reasons not to run. John hated excuses. Even if I was sore I never told John I couldn't run. I always gave it my all. He saw me put everything I had left into the part of the training I hated the most.

One of the days after running I could feel my hamstring getting abnormally tight. It was painful, and I felt the need to grab on to hold it together or it would come flying off. It hurt every time I had to step forward, and splits were excruciating.

I let it hurt for weeks before I decided I needed to tell a coach. I hated being injured, and I held off from telling John as long as I could bear it to avoid having to miss practices to recover. I finally told him that I was in pain, where it hurt, and what it hurt to do. I remember telling him because it was the first time I had told John that I was in pain, and I was scared to disappoint him. I remember the way he looked at me when I was telling him and being surprised when he looked genuinely concerned.

Then I made the mistake of telling him that it had been hurting for quite some time, and he turned angry.

"Rachel. Why didn't you tell me right when it started hurting? Now it might be ten times more serious because you kept using it. Go stretch and ice."

Honestly, I think this was the very first time John was upset with me. I was truly working through it because I didn't want to disappoint him, but it backfired. I was never someone who faked pain to get out of doing assignments, and it made him believe me when I told him something hurt. He immediately sent me to see our team doctor.

He sent me to see Larry Nassar.

This was the first time of many times I would see Larry for my injuries. Before this, I had only heard of the magical doctor who healed the worst injuries. People said he had the kindest heart and was a saint in a gym full of powerful and intimidating figures. He listened to your problems and always took your side, even if it was against John. People described him as unimaginably selfless. He sacrificed his time every Monday night to come see Twistars gymnasts for free. He opened up his home, his office, and his training room to all of us at any point. From the outside, he seemed an angel.

Larry sent me for an MRI that showed I had a torn hamstring. It was not bad enough to require surgery, but it would be an extensive amount of time off and numerous meetings for physical therapy.

Naturally, he volunteered to be my physical therapist.

Larry and I worked together for months strengthening my hamstring. My mom came often with me, but sometimes she was absent when I saw him at the gym. Larry came when practice was over on Mondays. Coaches and girls who didn't have injuries went home, and we stayed to get our so-called treatment.

"Treatment."

I would most regularly see Larry at the gym on Mondays. His training room at Twistars was small, doubling as a storage room for our recreational equipment. It smelled musty and sweaty, as we always saw him after a five-hour practice, so none of us were necessarily clean. People crammed into that tiny room even if he was "treating" someone so they could talk to him. There was absolutely no privacy. Both girls and boys saw Larry, and there was no curtain, no door, no separation from everyone seeing him perform his treatments . . . and he still did them.

Power of authority.

I was fourteen years old at this point. I was fourteen years old when Larry told me he was doing an "internal manipulation" on me. He told me pain in a tight hamstring can sometimes be lessened if the muscles around it are relaxed. He said this would require "internal massaging." He wasn't asking for permission to perform his treatment, he was more giving me a warning of what was coming. I still never said no. I didn't tell him to stop when I felt like I wanted to puke from discomfort. At fourteen years old, part of me knew something wasn't right, but I never told him I wasn't going to let him do it anymore.

I dreaded the days I had to see Larry because of the way he made my body feel. I worried about what he was thinking about. I was curious if he was judging my body. I told myself the typical statement we all tell ourselves when we have uncomfortable and vulnerable appointments with medical professionals: "He sees hundreds of girls; he won't remember my body." I told myself his power, credentials, prestige, and authority gave him the right to treat my body how he saw best for my injury. His power and authority trumped my comfort and ethics—another disgusting flaw in the culture of gymnastics. I know Larry remembers my body.

He continued to perform manipulations on me until my hamstring felt normal again a few months later.

Current men, women, and children who feel that their comfort is being sacrificed for authority figures, speak loudly.

I am so saddened by the fact that we live in a society that has an unclear line between what is morally okay and what is unacceptable. We live in a world where people have to question whether what just happened to them was considered abuse, assault, or rape because of stipulations of the situation. We find excuses for our abusers, for ourselves. We try to find ways out of having to admit we were assaulted, that we were a victim.

No, you are never drunk enough to make rape okay. No, your outfit was not revealing enough to make unwanted advances on you okay. No, there is not enough power and authority in the world to excuse assault and molestation.

Trust me, admitting and accepting that I was a victim of continuous sexual assault was the most difficult thing I have ever had to do. I was terrified of the consequences of using my voice, just as the other women who were abused by Larry were. We feared the attention, the pushback, the shaming that comes with voicing uncomfortable experiences. So many women do.

But we shouldn't.

I have heard the catcalls, had terrifying and unwanted advances made toward me, been inappropriately grabbed without consent and, because of Larry, molested. Many, many others have experienced what I have, and sadly, many more will. We need to fight it. We need to learn to recognize that any kind of discomfort produced by anyone is not acceptable.

Let nobody *silence the powerful voice that you have. Let* nobody *use your body a way that you have not approved of.*

Nobody.

Not strangers, not people you know, not people you love, not people who have authority over you. No amount of credentials, no length of a relationship, and no measure of experience gives someone a right to you or your body. The only person who has that right is you.

Stop finding excuses because you are afraid of the reactions. Stop ignoring advances that make you uncomfortable because you are afraid of the shaming that may come. Stop silencing yourself just to keep from having to admit you are a victim.

Because you aren't.

We are not toys for others to play with at their own leisure. We are not just objects and nothing more. We are not quiet sufferers. We are not victims.

We are survivors.

CHAPTER FOUR

~

Broken

Competition season at Twistars was so much different than the gym I was at before. It was much more structured and better organized. I felt more prepared for the first meet than I ever had before. I would be competing level 9 again, as my hamstring injury prevented me from getting the skills necessary to move up to level 10 during the summer training.

We flew through season and I triumphed at every meet I went to. I was representing my new team well, and I was proud of my accomplishments. My season was going extraordinarily. I was top ten in the national rankings for the entire year, dominating every meet I went to. I was having so much fun doing the sport I loved. Again I was the best, and I thrived off of it. At this point, I was a freshman in high school and had reached the age where colleges were starting to pay attention to me as a prospective scholarship athlete. I knew that how I did this and the following season would be crucial to my chances of getting a full-ride. I had started out the season in the best way I could have imagined. I was on everyone's radar. I received questionnaires from the top-recruiting schools because I was a National Champion at such a young age.

I was confident in my ability to obtain a scholarship.

My season was just as outstanding as the previous one had been. I defended my title at Nationals, and for the second year in a row, I stood at the top of the podium for the all-around. I swept the meet. In every event I was called back up to second- or first-place spot on the podium. I was so relieved. I had met every goal I set for myself. I met *my own* expectations. I truthfully do not think I have met the standards I set for myself since that moment. I always make them just slightly unrealistic. I live with a "shoot for the moon so you land among the stars" mind-set.

My parents sat quietly in the crowd watching the awards. Parents sitting directly behind them started gossiping after my name was mentioned for first place a few times. "What a sandbagger. Twistars does this a lot, you know. They put girls who should be in higher levels down in these lower ones just so they have more National Champions. Makes them look good. They don't think to give our girls a chance."

So much judgment. We got it from parents, from coaches, from colleges, and, of course, from the judges themselves. People thinking they knew our whole story before asking about it. People guessing the type of people we were from seeing us for such a short period of time. They guessed our personalities before they knew us. These parents didn't know I was out an entire summer with a torn hamstring, making it impossible to get the skills I needed for level 10. They forgot to think about how Twistars gymnasts might in fact train a little harder than their daughters. Maybe we ended up on the top of the podium consistently because of how hard we practiced and not by abusing the system.

Maybe the people who judged me are the reason I think even when I win there's a reason why I don't deserve it, that I still am not good enough.
Just a thought.

The summer following my second national title I trained extra hard. I was not going to be a level 9 again. I was letting people's judgment of my accomplishments scare me into training harder. I let people's excuses for my title push my training. I was going to be a level 10 in 2011.

I was a sophomore in high school, the peak age colleges recruit for gymnastics. Success at my first-year level 10 was vital. I visited a few campuses during this time and started to get a feel of what I was looking for in the college I would commit to. The key word here is *started*. I was fifteen. I had three full years left of growing up to do before I would even be at college, but I was expected to know what I wanted to commit to. I was expected to know where I wanted to spend four years of my life, three years ahead of time. It's extremely unrealistic for a sophomore in high school and a terrible characteristic of the culture of gymnastics. It forces us to peak our abilities at such a young age or a college scholarship is out of reach.

In the fall, John told me I could compete the first meet of the season as a level 10. This was huge for my goals and enormous for my confidence. John believed in me, so I believed in myself. Whenever John told me I could do something, I had no doubt that I could do it.

My first meet as a level 10 was phenomenal. I broke a 38.00 all-around score—a score some gymnasts never reach in their entire careers. College recruiting questionnaires poured into my e-mail. I was so happy. My love for the sport radiated through me. I was so proud of the gymnast I was becoming and so excited to see where the sport would take me. Success in my sport meant a healthy mental state and good amount of confidence in my skin for me.

John began to count on me as one of his most consistent competitors. Consistency was always my strength in gymnastics. I rarely fell, and I could always be relied on for a good score for the team. At one of the meets in my first season as a level 10, I was last in the lineup; there were some bad scores ahead of me and a lot was riding on how I performed my routine. John was very upset at his team's showing, and you could tell he was feeling pressure. Before I saluted, John came to me and said, "If you don't hit this routine, we will lose the entire meet."

He wasn't lying; we were doing terribly. He knew I was dependable and he was testing me to see if I was as reliable under pressure—a skill I am very appreciative to have as an adult. I saluted and did my routine like I always did. My mind said my cue words and my body followed like a puppet. I knew I always controlled how my routine was, no matter the situation. Losing or winning, my performance never changed. John celebrated with his famous whistle when I stuck my landing. He hugged me tight.

"Good job, sweetheart."

My season continued to be strong and consistent. I was always a tough competitor, even against the more experienced level 10s. I continued to complete the recruiting questionnaires that were sent to me, and kept "earn a college scholarship" at the top of my priority list. My performances were getting me closer and closer to reaching this goal, and with every meet I could feel myself getting more and more excited for my future.

As if life was waiting for the perfect time to change the future I was planning, emotional distress number two happened.

My back had been starting to ache shortly after the season began. It hurt mostly to bend forward, but not enough to complain to anyone but my parents. My mom had me taking medicine for it before practices. She continued to ask me if I wanted to get it looked at. Although it hurt, it wasn't enough to stop me from competing. I didn't want to know if anything was wrong. It was gradually getting worse, but I wasn't going to let it ruin the season that I was having. Ignorance was bliss.

It was a typical practice day at Twistars. We were training hard with two weeks before the Regional Competition. I knew I needed to qualify to Nationals if I had any hope of committing to a college the following year. John was coaching every deduction out of our routines. Practices were brutal and everyone was on edge.

A teammate of mine decided that this was the day she was going to tick John off with disrespect. She was falling on every routine and clearly had given up on completing the assignment for bars. She spent an extra long time in the chalk bucket just to irritate John more. She wouldn't look at him when he was giving her corrections and was ignoring John's threats to send her home.

John lost it.

"Everyone to the floor! We're gonna run."

And so we ran. For a long time. The girl who was to blame for this ran with such a disrespectful glare it even ticked me off. My body hurt so much; my muscles were so tired. My already aching back was getting stiffer. I was going to be extremely sore for the 8:00 a.m. practice we had the next morning.

As I predicted, I woke up in so much pain. I slathered Icy Hot on my body and resented the girl who was the reason behind the stiffness. I hoped she knew how mad the team was at her. I hoped she felt bad.

Knowing her, she probably didn't even care.

I started on beam that morning. Getting myself through the running warm-up was nearly impossible, and here I was about to do five beam routines. I looked at the line on the floor that I usually warmed up my skills on. I thought to myself, "If I don't warm up my skills on the floor, that's a few fewer times I have to move my stiff and sore body."

My life's biggest mistake. I wish with every ounce of my body I had just warmed up my skills on that stupid line.

I hopped on the beam to begin routine one. My body was so sore. I moved through the choreography and prepared for my first skill: a back tuck into a straddle jump full. My arms swung down below my body and I bent forward to create momentum for my flight.

I felt my lower back crack loudly as I bent forward. The muscles around my spine were so tight they felt like they had snapped me in half. I lost my breath.

My muscle memory took over and continued through the motions of the back tuck. My body flew up like it usually did for the skill, and my back cracked again in the air. It all happened so fast, but felt like it was in slow motion. I was upside down in the air above the beam. I knew my back was broken, but I still had to land. My feet hit the beam first, then my hands reached forward to grab it as I landed short. I crumpled to the ground below the beam. I let my body fall six feet into a heap on the mat, and my spine cracked and shifted one last time. I couldn't breathe.

John was at my side in seconds. I couldn't move; I couldn't stand up. He picked me up and I cried in pain. He hadn't seen me cry since my very first practice with him. He carried me to the floor; my teammate had already made a bag of ice.

My memory has since blocked out what happened after that moment.

The next thing I remember doing was driving to Larry's office at Michigan State. I remember sitting there while he tried to pinpoint the areas that were tender to the touch. I remember him "mmming" every time I said it hurt. He knew exactly what was wrong. He looked at me and said, "Do you want to go to Nationals?" I, of course, answered, "Yes." He then said, "Then we will wait until Nationals is over to get an MRI." He knew what an MRI would show, and he knew it would keep me from competing. I also knew what it would show. I was in denial that this was how my season was going to end. I refused to accept my injury and I ignored my pain. My parents trusted Larry's words and believed it when he said I was not putting myself in more danger if I kept training, that I would only be challenging my pain tolerance. My parents hated the idea of pushing through what was clearly a serious injury. I am so stubborn, and my parents knew they couldn't stop me.

Once I set my mind to something, nobody can stop me.

John knew I was hurting, and he also knew I wasn't going to stop training. He recognized the importance of this season from a college scholarship perspective, and he was not going to stand in the way of my finishing the way I wanted to. He also trusted Larry. He forced me to take a few days off of practice, and then let me come back to prepare for Regionals.

Honestly, my training was a medicated and adrenaline-filled blur. I was in an indescribable amount of pain, but it hurt more to think about taking time off to heal at this point in my season.

Larry volunteered to work with me again to get me through the end of season. In fact, he told me that the only way that I would finish the season was if I continued to work with him only, that every other doctor would force me to stop. I went into his room like I had for my hamstring injury, and he gave me the same talk about tight muscles in my groin area having effects on the pain around it. He told me I would again need his "internal manipulations" for my back injury. I remember thinking that it was weird. What did my muscles that low have to do with my injury in my spine?

But like every other girl, I trusted him and his treatments.

Again I dreaded appointments with Larry because I knew what they entailed. I started thinking about future sessions, and my fear of the discomfort grew with every visit. I knew this injury was bad and was going to take a lot of time off and rehab—a lot of sessions with Larry. I dreaded how the next few months would make my body feel discomfort beyond the shattered spine.

John reduced my numbers tremendously in practice. He wouldn't let me do a single floor routine, and he barely let me vault. He saw one good turn and made me get off the event. He had me visualizing routines thousands of times. He told me to do walk-through routines without the skills. He asked me to picture the sounds, smells, and feelings of the arena. He had me solidifying my cue words. He convinced me of the power of mental preparation. He told me that four mental routines is the equivalent to one physical routine with the way our brain stimulates the nerves during visualizations.

But I hated how unprepared I felt for a meet so important to my future. I walked into Regionals having yet to do a full floor routine because John hadn't let me. I had shooting pain down my legs that made every twist and turn extra excruciating. I saw Larry before the meet began. (Of course, he had volunteered to work the event as the trainer.) He threw some kinesio tape across my back, over my butt, and down my legs. He knew my back was fractured, but he wasn't about to upset one of his regular visitors by forcing me to stop and heal.

I was in my own world for Regionals. I ignored everyone. I focused on my one goal of getting to Nationals and I did the bare minimum. I started on vault. I went over the horse for warm-up twice compared to my usual four or five times. I saluted the judge and completed my vault.

I landed on my feet and that was good enough for John. He scratched me from competing my second vault.

Bars and beam were nothing above average. I didn't fall, and that met John's lowered expectations for me. I started to look around at the other gymnasts competing. I stared at vault and watched a girl stumble out of her landing. I looked over to bars and saw another gymnast cast over on a handstand.

I remember thinking, "Why is everybody falling?"

John came back to where I was waiting for my turn to start warming up for floor. He said, "Rachel, all you have to do to make it to Nationals is not fall in this routine. You need to fight to stay up." It seemed like everyone was having an off day, if what I was doing was good enough to qualify.

What John told me would have been comforting if it were anything but floor left. I hadn't landed a full routine on the event in almost three weeks. My legs were shooting with pain and my back felt like it was bruising itself with how hard it was throbbing. I looked at my parents in the crowd, and they looked so nervous. My mom smiled and my dad put his hands together to form a heart in front of his chest. They hated seeing me in pain, but they never stopped supporting me. They reminded me how loved I was no matter what happened on this last event.

I warmed up the bare minimum, as I could feel my medication wearing off. I felt my back start to seize and all of my ribs shift out of place to adjust to the tightened muscles that were trying to protect my fracture. Everyone knows what a rib out of place feels like, so you can imagine how all of them shifting incorrectly feels.

It was my turn next. "Just stay standing," I kept telling myself. "Two more minutes of pain, and then you're done." My mental toughness was strengthening by the second. I forced myself to ignore the pain, and my mind let me. My adrenaline surged through my spine and numbed it. I saluted, and my music began.

I stood in the corner to begin my first tumbling pass. Deep breath. My head started streaming through my cue words. "Push, hurdle, roundoff, back handspring, set, flip, flip, spot, stick." My body listened and performed what I had been visualizing hundreds of times. One pass down, two to go.

I pushed off the ground into my switch leap, and my feet landed together to rebound into my jump. "*Ouch!*" I screamed in my head as my rebound was slightly crooked and shot pain up through my spine and down my legs.

"Refocus, Rachel." My thoughts scolded me for thinking about my pain.

I stood in the corner and took a deep breath before my second pass. "Push, hurdle, roundoff, back handspring, set, twist hard, punch, flip, spot, stick." My two-and-a-half-punch front tuck put me on my feet again. Two passes down, one to go. I was almost done; I could feel it. One pass left. It would all be over in fifteen seconds. I got to the corner for my final pass and took one last deep breath.

"Run, push, hurdle, roundoff, back handspring, set, flip, flip, spot, stick."

"*Owwwwwww!*"

The landing of my last pass shot lightning bolts of pain throughout my entire body. My eyes started to water. I disregarded my practiced choreography that required me to do a few more movements around the floor and instead stayed planted where I landed, moving just my arms. It looked terrible, but I was done. I had qualified to Nationals. John was right next to me when I got off the mat and gave me a hug.

"Good job, sweetheart."

I looked to my parents again in the crowd. Mom smiled, and dad shot me two thumbs up. I could tell part of them hated that I had one more meet, that they would have to watch me push through my pain for two more weeks.

Part of me hated it, too.

While I was seeing Larry after the meet, I saw the other gymnasts who had qualified for Nationals go into a large room and come out with both arms filled with new gear to wear to Nationals. Bags filled with new sweatpants, sweatshirts, blankets, sunglasses, beach towels, and raincoats, all completely decked out in our region's logo and colors. This was so much more than what we had gotten in level 9. When I got to the room after "treatment," I realized that it was even more overwhelming than I had imagined. Twenty volunteers stood behind huge tables packed full of what we were about to be given. They sized us and threw things into our arms until they were full. They sized us for our beautiful National leos.

I shiver when I remember the amount of pain I was in at this point in my life. It affected everything that I did. I wish so hard that I hadn't been so focused on gymnastics and cared more about my future. As a teenager, we don't think about the long term. We don't see the consequences for tomorrow of our actions today. I didn't see how my decision to delay my diagnosis was idiotic.

CHAPTER FIVE

~

Diagnosis

John had me practice for Nationals the same way I prepared for Regionals—which meant barely practicing at all. I negotiated assignments with him. He agreed to let me do one floor routine before Nationals. He was always yelling at me for doing too much. I hated having him constantly upset with me. To be honest, I wasn't too fond of him either at this point. He wasn't letting me prepare the way I felt I needed to. He trusted my mental strength a lot more than I did.

John will never understand how much I appreciate now how he coached me then. Honestly, he may have saved me from not being able to carry my own children, losing control of my bladder due to nerve damage, or a lifetime of paralysis. He trusted Larry just as I did but somehow knew he needed to protect me further.

John's wife, Kathryn, also coached me at Twistars. She stayed primarily on beam. During this whole injury she found the perfect balance between letting me decide what I needed to do and limiting my assignments. We talked about my assignments every single day. I would warm up and go talk to her about what I thought I could do that day. Some days it was, "Kathryn, my pain meds are still working. I can do three routines." She would say, "You get two with your series in it, and one without."

(For those who are not well educated on the sport, a series on beam is the connected flips. My series was a back handspring back layout,

29

requiring a ton of arching. It was the most painful part of my entire beam routine.)

My compromises with Kathryn were perfect for me and made me feel as though I was in control of my training. John was trying to protect me physically and Kathryn was trying to prepare me mentally. They were puzzle pieces of a coaching staff that meshed incredibly together.

The team left for Nationals together, and now that I was with Twistars for good I stayed with them too. It was a full weekend of bonding, and I was officially a part of the robotic championship team. We went to the arena together to practice on the equipment the day before the meet. It was right when we got to the arena that John told me I couldn't flip that day. He said, "Go to all of the events and walk through your routines. Visualize them ten times. Imagine the smells and the noises for tomorrow. But do not flip."

I was so mad at him.

College coaches lined a wall sitting at huge tables, and boy, did I look like an untalented athlete just touching the equipment and waving my arms through a pretend routine. I hated the rule John gave me for the practice day. How were the colleges supposed to know to watch me tomorrow if I was just standing around today?

So many college coaches, from the best in the nation to Division III schools, were present, all taking notes and mingling with each other. It was incredibly intimidating. Once again in my gymnastics career, I was being judged on "worthiness." I hated this part of my sport. I hated how people drew conclusions about my talent based on how I did at one meet. People were determining my worth based on how I performed during three minutes.

That is not enough time to determine worthiness of a full-ride college scholarship.

I was questioning my worth as a sixteen-year-old because that's when adults were trying to determine it for me—yet another sickening part of gymnastics culture. I do not put the blame on the college coaches. If one college rebelled against the system and didn't recruit at such a young age, it would not stand a chance against the other schools that did. The entire system should be adjusted.

Let us grow up a little before you go putting a dollar amount on us.

During practice I saw the schools that had already sent me questionnaires. I knew my name was on their list to watch, and here I was doing absolutely nothing. How impressive. I felt annoyed and uncomfortable. I wanted to go back to the hotel for the entire hour, and I was honestly relieved when our allotted practice time was over.

The morning of Nationals I did my usual prep routine. My mom braided my hair and put it into a bun filled with three thousand bobby pins piercing my skull. She slipped me my lucky ice cream sandwich in secret, because if John knew that was what I was eating to fuel myself for a competition he would have lost his mind. He also would have disapproved of my dependence on a superstition. It was a tradition we thought best to keep a secret. I took my pain meds and walked to the arena.

I started on vault, same as Regionals. I wasn't going to do too many vaults in the warm-ups, just enough to feel ready. I stood on the blue felted runway as our warm-up began. My first time running to the vault I realized the step I usually take my hurdle on was way too far away from the horse than it should have been. My steps were completely off. The tape measure must have been a different distance from the horse than the one at my gym at home. I hadn't been allowed to get used to this tape measure during the practice day because of the stupid no flipping rule placed on me. Again, using different equipment in gymnastics is very difficult to adjust to. Everyone else knew their steps, since they had the day before to figure them out. Pure anxiety took over my body. Figuring out your steps takes at least four turns to feel comfortable before you're able to safely flip over the horse. I only had time for four turns down the runway total and only had the physical strength for two.

I had already wasted one of those two chances on realizing I had no idea what my steps were.

I ran down the runway again. My hurdle was way too close to the horse this time, but I went for it anyway.

Stupid.

My feet barely made it onto the springboard and I crashed onto the horse. My arms buckled on what should have been a back handspring onto the table, and the top of my head smashed into it from the missing support. I didn't go for the flip, but I still had the height and momentum to. My back landed flat on the mat hard after falling from nearly ten feet in the air. Smacking the mat with such force made a monstrous noise that echoed throughout the arena. All eyes were on me, watching as my eyes filled with water reacting to my fractured back crashing into the hard ground.

John helped me up. He didn't say anything. He didn't have to. I knew what he was thinking. He was mad I balked on my flip. If I had tucked and rolled my back would have been safe(er). He always told us to never balk because it was so dangerous.

"Are you good to compete or are we done?" he asked.

I nodded yes and said, "I'm competing."

My warm-up was over. The two times down the runway I was allowed were wasted and my body was nowhere near ready to compete. I walked back to the end of the runway and paced. I thought maybe I could walk off the pain. There were a few girls who had to compete before it was my turn, so I visualized. I knew two places I couldn't start my run. One was way too far away from the horse and the other was way too close. John could see my stress building up. He came to me, pointed to his temple and said, "Be tough up here, or don't go." He didn't want me to make another stupid mistake that would injure me even more. He reminded me how mentally strong I was. He reminded me to trust my mental training.

It was my turn. I walked up next to the runway and stood at the spot in between the two I had tried during warm-ups and failed at. I saluted the judges. The sound of the arena drowned out and I only heard the air inhale and exhale out of my nose for one final big breath. I ran, and my cue words streamed through my mind to match my body's movements. "Push, speed, too far from the horse . . . adjust, faster, hurdle, roundoff, block, twist, stick."

John clapped hard and whistled. He hugged me tight.

"Go sit down. We have some time before bars." I glanced over at the college coaches tables. They were all sitting today, taking notes and videotaping. There was no mingling; today was business. Today they were shopping for future investments.

Sixteen-year-old pieces of property.

Bars and beam went very well. I was proud of my performances and so was John. He got more and more excited as the meet progressed, but my pain was getting worse and worse. One more event and I would finally give in to my parents' nagging to get an X-ray. One more floor routine and I could rest for months. It was almost my turn to go, and John came up to me to give me the usual pep talk and correction reminders. Instead, this time he said something different.

"Rach, you are sitting in the top ten all-arounders going into this event." I felt myself smile big. "Show them what you got," he said.

My arms raised above my head for my salute. I stepped onto the floor and got set in my starting pose. My music began. Again, the arena drowned out. All I could hear was my music and my heartbeat increasing speed. I saw John on the side of the floor with his right hand extended tight like it always was for his gymnasts' routines. It was his way of staying tight for us. His chin was lowered and he was peering over the top of his glasses.

My body moved through the motions because of the power of my thoughts. I landed my floor routine because I relied on the distraction my cue words gave me. John hugged me so tight. I could feel both his pride and his relief that I was done. I think everyone was relieved. My season was over and it was time to heal. I had finished the season the way that I wanted to and even earned a spot on the National team by placing fourth in the all-around.

I proved my worth to everyone, including myself.

I left the meet exhausted—emotionally, physically, and mentally drained. I was so happy to be done, and I was beyond ready to heal. When I got home, I finally went to the hospital and got an X-ray and MRI. Sure enough, I had three fractures in my lumbar spine. I had felt right when each had individually happened. My MRI looked terrible. It had fractures everywhere, discs slipped forward, and discs bulging far into my spinal cord. The slipped discs were the likely cause of my back pain before the back tuck, but a month before, I had quite literally shattered my spine with one backflip.

I sat in the offices of the almost ten doctors I saw. I stared at my feet as they told me the same thing as the one I had seen before. My mom asked so many questions. My parents were there as I met with doctor after doctor, listening to my options. They heard all of them saying similar things.

"You need a very invasive spine fusion surgery that will make it impossible to come back to gymnastics."

"You have to quit gymnastics."

"You won't be able to control your bladder when you're thirty if you keep doing gymnastics."

I ignored them. I drowned out their words. They weren't what I wanted to hear, so I didn't listen. I was such a brat of a teenager. My parents absorbed everything and kept looking for more opinions. Maybe they kept looking because they knew I wasn't going to stop doing the sport that I loved. Or maybe they thought if I heard that I needed to quit from ten different doctors, I would listen.

But one doctor gave me another option. One doctor believed a comeback was possible. He told me it would be a long road to recovery, but that I could do it. I could continue to be a gymnast. I latched onto the words from one doctor and ignored the rest.

That one doctor was Larry.

I remember sitting with him at his clinic office. We looked at my MRI in his corner room filled with windows. There were signed pictures of Olympians and famous gymnasts filling his walls. All were autographed with personalized messages of gratitude. In the bunches of pictures was the picture of Kerri Strug's famous broken-legged vault to win the Olympics for Team USA. There Larry was, carrying her off the vault runway. They made me feel hopeful when my MRI was flashed up on his computer. He scrolled through the images, pausing after each movement to analyze the damage. He "hmmed" and nodded through the X-rays. He looked at me and jokingly said, "Well, it's no wonder your legs hurt!" and chuckled to himself.

How did he make me feel comforted in such a dreadful situation?

He then asked to look at my movements. He had me bend forward and arch back, and he traced my spine to track the shifting. He assured me that he couldn't feel it moving, and that it was most likely stable where it was. He assured me it wouldn't get worse as I kept doing gymnastics.

Here he was again, building my connection to him . . . my draw to him.

Like the other doctors, Larry explained to me the warning signs to look out for as I continued gymnastics. He told me that my big toe is a huge point of reference to determine the health of my back. He said I should always be able to lift it, and that it was okay if it was weak or numb.

I was such an idiot for thinking that that was okay.

Over the past few months, I have been heavily reflecting on this time in my life, questioning everything. At that point, Larry's opinion meant the world to me, and he knew it did. He gave me hope when everyone else was trying to rip it away from me. He gave me happiness when I was being swallowed by depression. He believed in me when nobody else did. He knew my potential, and he trusted that I could reach it.

Or did he?

*Looking back now, I am **repulsed**. Larry clearly had ulterior motives to encourage my comeback. For one, it was a lower back injury. These injuries were consistently a ticket to his "internal manipulations." My injury was bad enough that it was going to require almost a full year of his "treatment" . . . a full-year subscription to his "services." He had already performed his manipulations on me for my hamstring, so he knew I was a quiet target. I hadn't brought attention to my discomfort before, so why would I be a dangerous victim now?*

His sick mind probably thought, "Jackpot."

He told me I could do it because he wanted to continue to use my body for his own personal pleasure. He knew I would hang on to his belief in me. He knew I trusted him. The thought disturbs me to my core. I often think about how much danger he put me in, how willing he was to sacrifice my entire future for himself. One bad turn, and I wouldn't be able to walk. One wrong landing, and the possibility of carrying my own children would have been erased. The man I once viewed as a selfless saint I now see as a self-indulgent monster.

Larry sent me to get my torso fitted for a cast. Since it was my lower spine that needed to be immobile, they molded a cast that covered from my ribs to just over my butt. It was a hard plastic that felt like a constant waist trainer. I couldn't bend forward to tie my shoes, and sleeping in any position besides on my back was impossible. The brace was dreadful. I went nights without sleeping because I couldn't get comfortable. I had permanent bruises on my hips and ribs from the corner of the plastic. I could feel my stomach grow as I ate and didn't work out, because the plastic would get tighter. I could adjust the size of the cast, but my confidence in my body decreased to a new disgusting low every time I had to make it bigger to fit my body.

It makes me so sad to remember thoughts I had about myself at this point in my life. At sixteen years old, I was disgusted by my figure. I had arm muscles as big as a male weightlifter. My shoulder muscles were bulging instead of being lean like a normal woman. It was all okay when I had abs to accompany the other muscles, but as those faded because of my inactivity, I grew to despise my appearance.

I wish I could go back and tell myself that I was beautiful.

I think about how I feel about myself now. Honestly, not much has changed since I was sixteen because I still hate how I look. As my muscle tone fades, so does the shred of confidence I have left. I hate mirrors. But I'll bet in ten years I will want to go back in time and tell the woman I am now that I am beautiful, just like I want to with my sixteen-year-old self.

As this injury happened in the end of April, it was also near the end of the school year. I went to school every day with that stupid brace on. I did a great job at hiding it under my sweatshirts for a while. Baggy clothes took over my wardrobe because I was so embarrassed by my turtle shell of a brace. Eventually, it got too warm out to wear sweatshirts. Even more so, our school was about to host Honors Week. This was the seniors' last week at school before they finished early. The week was filled with cute sundresses, awards, scholarship presentations, and honors recognition. I couldn't wear a sundress. I could barely wear jeans with my low confidence.

I threw on leggings for Honors Week. This was tighter than I wanted to go, but I needed to dress at least half decently. Everyone would be dressed up and I didn't want to stand out too much and draw attention to my cast. I walked into school and through the hallway where all of my friends gathered on the first day of Honors Week. They all looked so dressed up. One of my guy friends yelled, "Rach! You're not even going to dress up for spirit week!?"

All eyes were on me as my cheeks and chest turned red and starting burning. Anxiety started raging through my veins. My brain shut down.

"I can't fit into my nice clothes. My brace . . ." was all I could get out.

I lifted my baggy T-shirt to reveal the huge white plastic shell I had over my growing belly. My friend felt terrible, I know he did. "Oh jeeze . . . I . . . I'm sorry, Rach." My eyes started to water, and I didn't want him to see how much he had hurt my feelings. It was an honest accident. I should have been in nice clothes; it was almost a policy in our school to dress up during Honors Week. I went to the bathroom and cried.

Although I put on jeans and a nice shirt for the remainder of Honors Week to fit in better, my comfort in my skin was even lower than on the first day.

CHAPTER SIX

~

Unworthy

Practices with a broken back flat-out sucked. They felt like a waste of time. I watched as all of my teammates transitioned from event to event, training new skills and upgrading their routines. My gymnastics continually got worse because of inactivity as theirs got better. My competitiveness burned inside me.

To make things worse, all of the colleges that I had gotten attention from because of my performance at Nationals were coming in to watch me "practice." Granted, they were coming in to recruit a few girls at Twistars, but I knew I was on their notes to keep an eye on and report back to the head coach about. I wonder how they worded what my practice looked like to them. I brainstormed possibilities about what they were writing as I stretched for five hours.

I bet they wrote, "Immobile."

I imagined some said, "Crippled."

For sure one or two put, "Broken."

I imagined them all saying, "Unworthy."

So disgusting. Here I was feeling unworthy again as a sixteen-year-old because of my sport . . . because of my sport's culture . . . because of every sport's recruiting culture. I fell into depression as my identity slowly slipped away from me because of my injury.

John was selling me the best that he could. He told the colleges about my work ethic, my respect for coaches, my consistency, and my motivation to recover better than ever. Some believed him, and some dropped me off of their recruiting list so fast I didn't even have my cast off yet.

Honestly, I love people who don't believe in me. I feed off of people who tell me I am incapable of doing something. Every college that deemed me a "risky recruit" because of my injury was fueling my fire to come back and prove them wrong.

Qualifying to be on the team from Nationals meant two things: one, that John would reward his three gymnasts who had qualified with a suite-view Justin Bieber concert, and two, that I got to attend the most prestigious camp in the nation. That summer, I traveled down to Texas to attend the camp with the other gymnasts who had made it. Back brace and all, I landed at the Karolyi Ranch. The best trained here. Every gymnast who was ever at the Olympics trained in this gym, stayed in the cabins, and used this equipment. I felt so honored to be there. I couldn't do anything because I was injured, but I was still so happy to have made it to such a prestigious place.

I ended up being a little grateful I was injured because the practices looked terrible. The girls were forced to do endless workouts with few breaks, even for water. We all were crammed onto equipment meant to house twelve gymnasts, not the group of fifty that was there. The gym was sweltering hot, and I was dripping with sweat just doing rehab. I felt pressured to continue to make people think I was worthy of being there, even though I had already qualified to be there. It was sickening. The culture of gymnastics continued to make me feel like what I did wasn't good enough even through what was supposed to be a reward.

I personally experienced the cabins that had no cell phone service. I saw that the only male allowed in our cabins was Larry. I was in the training room that so many were abused in. I ate in the cafeteria and experienced the way they forced us to eat so little and so healthy for the week. I saw the disgusting way they thought we should be treated. I was controlled in ways I shouldn't have been.

I traveled to a few places that summer that felt like they had the power to control and belittle, which made me reevaluate my worthiness. I traveled all the way down to one college, toured the campus, met the team, and saw the gymnastics training facility for a program that had been heavily recruiting me since I had won my first Nationals in level 9. After the entire day of activities for this program that showed a serious intention to offer me a scholarship since I was fourteen, I sat down to meet with the coaches. They bluntly described how they felt about my injury.

"You're a great risk for this program. A risk we are no longer willing to take."

I heard that from a few places where I had been on the recruiting radar for before my injury. I watched as my dreams of continuing gymnastics in college faded away. I saw all of my hard work, accomplishments, and everything that I had pushed through to meet my goal be rendered unimportant. Nobody was seeing how motivated I was to come back. Nobody paid attention to my willingness to push through pain to succeed. People only saw the terrible injury. People only saw me as damaged property that wasn't worth investing in.

Because, remember, college gymnastics is just a business, and gymnasts are just employees.

I was getting more and more upset with college coaches as more and more discontinued interest in me because of my injury. Many had given up on me, but a few remained. I had a strong list of five colleges that had come and watched me "practice" and hadn't removed me from their list of candidates for a scholarship. Three of those five were in the Big Ten. I started to accept that this conference was most likely where I would be headed. The top-ranked SEC (Southeastern Conference) schools that had previously shown great interest had all crossed me off their list in thick Sharpie.

I remember the day Minnesota came in to watch me "practice." It was toward the end of summer, so I was well into my recovery. Larry told me that day I was cleared to hang from the bar. This seems tiny, but this was a huge advance in my training options. Hanging opened the door for pull-ups, dips, wrist work, and hanging routine visualizations. I was on the bars for the full five hours the day Minnesota was in watching. I was in such a good mood with my new clearance to hang. The bar in my hands felt so good. I was radiating happiness while my hands blistered and ripped from the forgotten feeling of the bars.

Minnesota asked me to come on an unofficial visit. This was promising. Finally, a move forward from a school in the recruiting process. I had visited many schools before, but I was excited about this visit. I had visited another school a few weeks earlier and gotten a full-ride scholarship offer, but the university wasn't giving me the feeling that I belonged there.

I was hopeful Minnesota would.

My trip to Minnesota started out terribly. For one, my boyfriend at the time and I decided to break up my first night we were in Minneapolis. From that point, I had already concluded that bad things happened at Minnesota and felt the state was radiating bad vibes. I didn't sleep at all and was exhausted when I had to get up at 6:00 a.m. to begin my day touring Minnesota's campus. Second, I was missing a big test in one of my classes. My teacher was lenient, letting me take it when I got back, but things like this were life-ending issues as an anxiety-filled teenager.

Two strikes for the University of Minnesota before I had even stepped foot on campus.

I walked onto campus with a predrawn conclusion that I wasn't going there. Being the dramatic teenager that I was, a breakup meant my world had stopped spinning and college was unimportant compared to the drama I was going through.

But Minnesota's campus worked its magic extra hard for me.

The campus is stunning. If you have never been there, I highly suggest it. It's a cute and kept-up college town planted just outside two enormous cities. "Dinkytown" was where my tour started. The gymnastics training facility and athletic facility were located just a few blocks apart, with the tiny town in between. We parked our car and started to walk to meet the gymnastics coaching staff and observe practice. The tiny town made me smile. It looked like a fun place to go, even as a sixteen-year-old. A cute little ice cream parlor sat on the corner of the street opposite the gymnastics facility. My parents and I walked past it as a car of four college students came rolling by with the windows down and heads out of the window belting "Pumped Up Kicks." Their joy was contagious, and it made my grumpy teenage self happy.

I walked into the gym. It was small and quaint. The gym used to be a classroom building with a school gym upstairs, but somehow they had organized the space in a way to fit all of the gymnastics equipment. Everything was super close, but it also looked safe. I was met by the head coaches and assistant coach who had traveled to watch me practice at Twistars. They introduced me to the team as they started strolling in from class. I was very quiet and did my best to talk as little as possible. I am quite the introvert, but I can play extrovert when I have to. It's just exhausting. I hadn't slept at all the night before, so forcing myself to be "on" that day was impossible.

I sat and watched the girls warm up. They looked like they meshed together so well, but they clearly had extremely different personalities. The coaches said, "Let's warm up!" and instead of circling up and running like every other team I had watched did to warm up—along with my own—the girls spread out and started dancing. Loud music pumped through the gym as the girls danced synchronized aerobics. The head coach came over to me and said, "We do this at meets for our warm-ups too. It's more fun than just running, and loosens everyone up better than jogging."

"That's awesome," I remember thinking.

The routine they did looked so cool, and the music was fun and upbeat. They knew a ton of different routines. Apparently they learned a new one for competition season every year, and so they had a memorized a lot throughout their four years as they continued to pass down the moves and teach incoming freshmen.

Practice looked relaxed and enjoyable compared to my club gym. The girls picked their assignments since it was in the off-season, and even got to pick which events they went to at which times. It was like they had open gym for practice every day. I wondered, "What the heck kind of dream gym is this?" They got to play gymnastics for as long as they wanted, and got to leave whenever they were done. One gymnast left after just the aerobics, telling the coach, "I have a test tonight I have to study for," and the coach just said, "Sounds good!" I couldn't hide my wide-eyed and raised-eyebrow reaction to that interaction. I was in total and complete shock. I thought it was fake, that she was acting so calm just to impress me. No way did that just fly like that. No way.

After practice, I toured campus and met with a ton of different people I don't even remember. I was exhausted and darn near falling asleep in my seat listening to them tell me about college academics three years before the information would be relevant to me. It was just for my parents, and my brain was shutting down because of it. I met with academic advisers, tutors, counselors, trainers, and even the academic adviser for the major I was interested in, speech and language pathology. (This wasn't even close to the degree I ended up getting.)

We went back to the gym the next day to watch a morning practice before going to the football game. We went shopping at the Gopher Gear store to pick up a Minnesota shirt to fit into the crowd before practice began. The coaches brought me onto the field to stand close enough to smell the sweat on the players during their warm-ups. I felt so small compared to the six-foot giants with massive amounts of padding. I even got to stand in the student section with the gymnasts for the game. I thought it was strange how the girls had just spent so many hours during the week together in the gym and were choosing to hang out outside of practice, too. "They must be such a close team," I continuously thought.

They did an outstanding job at making my stupidly quiet self feel included. They asked me questions and tried to get to know more than just my surface characteristics. I felt like they actually cared about who I was as a person and not just the amount of athletic success I would bring to their team.

Once the game was over, we walked back to the gym to meet with the coaches. I was about to fly back home, and they wanted to spend time with me before I left, talking to me about how I felt my visit to see them went. We talked about the facilities, the resources I would have through the athletic department to assist me with my academics, competition season, and what they were looking for in the recruits they wanted at Minnesota.

"We have a specific culture we aim to uphold," the head coach said. "We want girls that bring us the whole package, and not ones that are just talented in the sport. We look for good students and great character. We care most about work ethic, coachability, and passion for the sport."

The assistant coach who had seen me at Twistars chimed in next.

"I have never seen someone who was so limited by an injury do so much . . . and be so excited about it," she said. "You did not stop smiling for the entire five hours I watched you practice, and you barely got off that bar. It was unbelievable to watch. I got to see your personality and love for the sport even when you are battling through a serious injury comeback."

"That is why we want you at Minnesota," the head coach said. "We want to offer you a full-ride scholarship to our university because your character matches the culture we have built and intend to keep."

I left the campus I had come to with negative predrawn conclusions with an enormous smile on my face and a sense of certainty in my heart. I knew this was where I was supposed to be.

The University of Minnesota was supposed to be my home.

CHAPTER SEVEN

~

Medicated

I verbally committed to the University of Minnesota about a month later. The weight that was lifted from my shoulders was indescribable. I had found a college that still wanted me regardless of an injury, a college that cared about more than just my talent, a college that believed in me.

I was slowly working back from my injury. Larry was gradually letting me do more and more gymnastics as he continued to work with me as my "physical therapist." I was seeing him every Monday, and sometimes one or two more times a week either at his house or at his office at Michigan State University. He was always more than willing to work on me whenever I needed him.

Wonder why.

The closer the season got, the more frequently I was cleared to do new skills. Every week I would come excruciatingly early to practice to be the first to sign up to see Larry and be cleared to do more skills. It started with the small things like hanging and running, and eventually I was allowed to bounce on a trampoline and do cartwheels and round-offs. Midway through the preseason, I was allowed to try aggressive flipping like back tucks and front tucks. When I tried them, I realized that they still hurt just as much as the year before.

But I refused to tell anyone.

The season was quickly approaching and I was just getting out of my brace and being cleared to do full gymnastics. I ran for hours for endurance. I lived on the low beam, relearning my skills as quickly as I could. I took as many turns as John and Larry let me. I was capitalizing on every clearance I got from Larry. I fed off everything he told me. I did everything he asked of me so he would believe I was ready to move to the next step of recovery. I was obeying him because he held all of the power to control what I was allowed to do. I was his obedient puppet.

Absolutely repulsive. I wish I could go back and protect the child I was. Shield myself from his repulsive treatments. I wish I could fight for the little girl I was, because nobody else knew that they should have been fighting for her.

I remember the day Larry cleared me to try everything again. Like everything else I had been cleared to do before, I overdid it. I did one thousand of everything he let me do. I made sure my body relearned how to sense where I was in the air. I retaught myself how to land, how to be aware of where my body was at all times. I never stopped moving. Slowly but surely, I was starting to prove everyone wrong, and I loved it.

I was still in pain, don't get me wrong. I was still feeling pain doing daily activities like standing, sitting, climbing stairs, and sleeping. I started to adjust my lifestyle to match the needs of my back pain. My back hurt bad enough to bring me to tears, but I was done with my time off. I was done with being limited. I was over continuously falling below the standards I had for myself. My mental health was at dangerously low levels and I was sick of it. I was ready for change. I could feel myself crawling out of the hole of depression the more I was cleared to do by Larry. Larry controlled my feelings just as he controlled my body. He had total and complete power over me, and I didn't even realize it.

Meet season was here and I was just being cleared to do gymnastics again. Nine months of recovery. It was supposed to be a year, but since I was being so obedient with my therapy Larry rewarded me.

Like a pet.

Looking back, I really don't think it would have mattered when I came back. It was going to be just as dangerous and risky after two years as it was after nine months. I tried getting my skills back as fast as I could. I was seeing the benefits of doing all of the visualizations John made me do. They were working. My skills came back easily, and I was able to put my routines together much quicker than anyone had predicted.

Step one of proving people wrong, complete.

I trained as hard as I could have to prepare for this season. I was pushing through so much pain, and John could see it. He limited my numbers often and sometimes wouldn't even let me onto an event. He could read me like a book. He knew when my back was having an extra sore day.

"Go stretch, Rach. No bars today."

Kathryn and I continued our compromising agreement that we had used before Regionals and Nationals the previous year. I began to be more honest with myself, knowing it was a long season ahead. I would tell her when I wasn't feeling well enough to do any series at all, even though it killed me to lose a day of preparation. I valued our trusting relationship, but it required me to be honest when the pain was too bad.

I hopped into competing midway through the season. It felt so good to put my competition leo on again. I hated missing even a few meets of the season because there were only about ten total every year. Missing meets meant missing opportunities to win, and we all know how that irked me. My back often throbbed from pain, and the feeling in my legs shifted from shooting pain to moments of numbness after doing certain skills. I preferred the shooting pain. The feeling of having numb legs is indescribable. The first thing to lose feeling was the top of my feet. I could run my hands along them and feel nothing. It was like they had fallen asleep without tingling. I had extreme difficulty lifting up my big toe, and if someone pushed it down I had no ability to fight it. I was slowly but surely developing a dragging foot as the disc bulging into my spinal cord continued to block the nerves that were responsible for giving it control and feeling. The nerves were slowly dying.

Why didn't that scare me? The things the doctors had told me as warning signs were happening, but I wasn't paying attention. I was still following Larry like a dog.

I tried everything to give my legs enough sensation to feel safe doing gymnastics. I started with putting Icy Hot cream on them every hour. Slowly that stopped being enough, so I would wrap them just a little bit too tight with tape so it was painful enough to make me feel it. Then I started putting Icy Hot patches under that tight tape. By the time I got to college, I was opening my pores with hot water and then putting an Icy Hot patch on them so it sizzled.

Healthy, right?

The season flew by, and it felt like I blinked and Regionals was already here. I guess that is what you get when you are injured for all of summer, preseason, and the first few meets. I felt a lot of pressure at the Regionals. There is already the pressure to qualify to Nationals, but I was adding onto that my personal desire to shove in everyone's faces that they thought I wasn't going to be able to come back. I wanted to beat all of my scores and places from last year. I added stress to myself that I shouldn't have.

I remember walking into Regionals. I was now a junior in high school, and this meant colleges came to Regionals to watch my age group to grab any last-minute potential investments that had previously flown under the radar. Some of the colleges there were ones that had slammed the recruiting door in my face. The college that had brought me onto campus just to tell me that I was unworthy was there too.

Cue the anxiety.

I started on beam that year. Beam was the hardest for me to do because of my stupid numb legs. Balancing on four inches is hard enough as it is, and trying to do it on legs that you couldn't feel was terrifying. I would slap my legs before turns as if they needed to be woken up. They didn't need to have their eyes opened—I did. I should have realized how dangerous this was. My ambition and competitiveness were blinding me into stupidity.

I approached the beam for my routine with so much self-placed pressure on my shoulders. I didn't want to succeed for myself, or even really to qualify to Nationals. The one goal that was burning inside of me above all others was just to prove wrong everyone who had doubted me. I didn't want to win to make myself happy; I wanted to win to make everyone else feel bad for turning me away. I looked at the beam with pure rage, like it represented everyone who had a part in shattering my dreams of being a college gymnast.

Salute. My stream of words began.

"Breathe, smile, pose, prepare." My arms raised to begin my series. They swung forward to give me momentum, and I could feel my legs shake as they fought for strength and feeling. "Hand hand, foot foot, set, foot . . ." My series was way off. I could feel my second foot fly over me at a completely wrong angle. I wasn't going to land even close to on the beam. I was going to fall. Every gymnast knows when they are

year, I was just as excited to qualify as I was the first year as a level 10. I could feel John's relief. I could tell my parents were much more relaxed. They knew I had accomplished what I wanted to, and it made them happy to see me happy. They all knew how hard I had worked for this moment.

I knew I had an amazing opportunity in my hands. Performing in front of the panel of colleges again at Nationals was exactly what I wanted. I wanted to show them what they had given up on and make them regret it. I wanted to teach them a lesson so that they wouldn't give up on future gymnasts just because they were injured. I hoped it would make them see us as people instead of pieces of property. There was so much motivating me through the two weeks of practices leading up to Nationals.

The arena at Nationals was huge that year. They were hosted in Virginia, and the location was stunning. It was so much warmer than it was where I was from in Michigan. Practice day in the arena was much better than the year before since John actually let me practice. I went to get my steps on vault first—must have been some PTSD coming to the surface.

While warming up I scanned the college coaches panel. Since it was practice day, none of them were in their seats behind their nameplates; they were all mingling. I was still able to spot my future coaches at Minnesota. I may have been biased, but they looked so much nicer and classier than any of the other coaches. Part of me was happy to see them so that I could have the chance to show them that I was worth the scholarship they had awarded me.

Part of me was terrified I would show them that I wasn't.

My spine felt my nerves the morning I woke up for Nationals. I could feel my muscles tighter than usual, squeezing the fractures in my spine. I took a larger dose of my pain meds than I usually did, my mom put my hair in the bobby-pin-filled bun, and I ate my superstitious ice cream sandwich. The Regional-qualifying team got ready and traveled to the arena together. We were one big clump of geared-up gymnasts.

Before warm-ups had even started, the college coaches were in their seats and already taking notes, organizing which coach was to keep an eye on which gymnast. I always felt like a state-fair animal at Nationals. We pinned numbers to our back like auction items and performed for the colleges to purchase us. Again, we were made to feel like property instead of humans. Instead of looking for people, the coaches were in charge of searching for our numbers. In my case, since I already had been "purchased," I knew Minnesota was watching to make sure I was a good investment. A show animal performing for them. They even went so far as to mark us as "purchased" or not with different colored dots on our numbers.

I hope I was not the only one to be sickened by the feeling of being an auctioned animal.

We did our running and stretching warm-up in a hidden gym behind a curtain. This was also where we had our warm-ups on the events. I always hated this. For one, we were warming up on completely different equipment from what we would be competing on, and we all know how good I was with switching equipment. It also meant that college coaches didn't see 75 percent of the gymnastics we did that day. They were judging our capabilities, our talent, and our worth from 25 percent of a competition. I can't imagine my parents liked it either, because they couldn't see me. They couldn't make sure I was okay, couldn't read my face to see how much pain I was in, couldn't gauge whether to shape a heart with their hands or give me two thumbs up. They were only seeing 25 percent of the meet, too.

Every time I walked from the warm-up gym to the competition gym I would try to find my parents. It was always comforting to see them in the stands before I competed. I think connecting with eye contact after the warm-up gym comforted them also.

To be completely honest, I don't remember much from this meet since I had taken a large dose of pain medication beforehand. I wouldn't want to give false feelings from my meet just because I don't remember exactly how each routine went like I do with some meets. I would end up finishing ninth in the nation that year. This wasn't better than my fourth place finish the year before, but I know that it was good enough to accomplish what I wanted to. I had impressed Minnesota and made other colleges question why they were so quick to turn me away.

CHAPTER EIGHT

~

All on the Floor

Seasons as a gymnast blend together. After you compete for twenty years, meets don't stand out in memory unless something happened at them. Many of my meets stood out because I was in so much pain, so I am happy that the summer following my junior year in high school is hard to remember—it means nothing traumatic happened. It was my senior year and my last summer with Twistars. John had given me a new sense of leadership and encouraged me to be a source of guidance for the gymnasts younger than me.

I give credit to John for instilling in me the leadership skills I have today. He was always reminding his older gymnasts how many little ones were looking up to them, watching them, and copying them. This encouraged me to be a leader even outside of the gym. I knew younger gymnasts followed me on social media, so I had a "professional"-looking profile even at seventeen. I know my leadership style is more of a "lead by example and guidance" than it is "direct and dictate," and I give credit for that to John. I also knew I needed to be professional because, as my parents were good at reminding me, Minnesota was always looking and could easily take my scholarship away. (I would see this power they held on my official visit when they took the full-ride away from a gymnast who broke their team rules and exhibited behavior that didn't match their culture.)

Looking back, this final summer at Twistars flew by, and it was already season again. I had such high expectations for my final season as a club gymnast. My visualization skills had been perfected from being injured for so long, so I started to get creative with them. I started to visualize myself in pressure sets. Before every beam routine, I would visualize myself in college in a maroon-and-gold leotard. I visualized us against another Big Ten rival and needing my score to win. I went into every practice routine adding extreme pressure to myself. I wanted to be just as consistent no matter the situation I was in, and I started preparing for it in my senior season.

This was the summer John let the seniors lead the horrendous running that we did every summer. I liked this new power he gave us, as it made me feel like I had a new motivation to do the running that I didn't have before. I even remember some days John would come and ask me how my body felt, and I would be honest and say that it was sore from a new conditioning list we were trying. He always believed me, and sometimes even told the entire team not to run that day because of my honesty. John's trust in those who respected him was unmissable.

That September, the other seniors and I signed our letters of intent to the colleges where we would continue our gymnastics careers. We had one senior going to UCLA to be on the coaching staff, three would compete at Western Michigan, one went to Ohio State, and I went to Minnesota. We all confirmed that our time with gymnastics wasn't over, and John once again had gotten a full class the opportunitiy to continue at a college level.

I loved the class that I graduated with. Together, we were a group of solid leaders who meshed wonderfully. We had bonded so much that we planned a trip to Disney together after the conclusion of our final meet the next season. We had been through everything together. One of the girls had even broken her back at the same time as me. We did rehab together, stretched together, and saw Larry together.

My back still throbbed during every practice, and my legs continued to get more and more numb. Larry kept encouraging me and kept working with me. I continued to see him every Monday even though I was doing 100 percent of my practices. He had informed me that continuing to see him would be vital to maintaining the pain level I had and not letting it get any worse. He told me that my sessions with him had transitioned from healing therapy to preventive measures. He warned me that if the treatments stopped, my back would hurt worse. He told me that if this happened, I would no longer be a gymnast. I was questioning why the therapy stayed the same when it was meant for a different purpose, but my fear of losing gymnastics outweighed every discomfort I had. Larry was still willing to work with me through my pain, so I was willing to push past how he made me feel. He was fighting to keep me as a regular visitor.

A consistent quiet victim.

I loved the final season of my club career. Truthfully, I think I peaked here. I was unstoppable. My scores were the highest they had ever been, and I won events and all-around frequently. Through eight meets, I was undefeated on floor. I think this was the one event I always wanted to excel at. Ever since my first level 9 Nationals, where I felt so belittled because of the simplicity of my floor routine, I wanted to go the extra mile on it. My routine was very difficult senior year, and I loved it. I loved having three impressive passes. I was prepared to train hard enough to end my career standing on the top of the podium at Nationals for it. I wanted to prove my twelve-year-old self wrong.

Going into Regionals this year, I was ranked number one in the nation for all-around. I was on the very top of the list for top level 10s in the nation. The cherry on top. My ranked all-around was a 38.675. When the rankings were posted that week, my classmates at school paid attention to me and recognized my talent. My closest friends and a few fans of the sport had previously recognized that I was talented, but the rest hadn't paid attention since I wasn't an athlete at the school. I didn't participate in sports for my school, so how would they know I was an athlete at all?

I actually barely even went to school. I was taking two online college-level courses for Post Secondary Enrollment Options and took two classes at the high school my senior year. My friends barely saw me because I had to adjust my schedule to make it to my practices at Twistars. I was basically half homeschooled. I didn't keep up with the drama at high school because I was never there to hear about it. I didn't get to go to football games because I had practice Friday nights, and I wasn't there after school for social hour because I was already at practice. I feel like a lot of people didn't even know I existed. If they did, it was only because my dad was the superintendent and I was the one who posted first about snow days.

I felt like these rankings made people understand my talent, my worth. Not just my high school, but the college coaches—Minnesota and the ones who turned me away. This was confirmation that I had proved the ones who turned me away wrong. I had tangible evidence of my comeback, and I still wasn't done.

Going into Regionals, I was number one in the nation and undefeated on floor. Twistars hosted Regionals this year, and Minnesota was hosting Nationals. How coincidental! My final two meets seemed to represent my transition from club to college. I felt like God was setting it up just for me. He built me the stage and all I had to do was perform.

I walked into Regionals and could feel eyes on me. Eyes were always on Twistars when they walked into an arena. I could feel the pressure and expectations people were placing on my shoulders because of my rankings and accomplishments during the regular season.

Maybe I was just putting them on myself.

I would be starting on vault, which meant ending on floor. I would have to let the pressure and nerves build up on every event before I could get them off my shoulders. My other events were consistently average and I would be ending with my best finale. I felt eyes watching me at every turn. Every parent there was waiting for me to make a mistake so his or her daughter could take my place. I think the pressure to remain at the top is more difficult to handle than the pressure to get there in the first place. Once you win, people know you can. Once you win consistently, people expect you to continue winning. This was exactly what I had prepared for in my visualizations. I had prepared for this amount of extreme pressure. I felt ready.

I stood at the end of the runway. Salute. Cue words: "Push, fast, hurdle, strong, block, tight, spot, land, stick."

Shooting pain combined with numbness in certain areas took over my legs. One event done, three to go. Parents watched like hawks as I revealed my weakness by sitting down in between turns and rubbing my back. They saw me slather layers and layers of Icy Hot on my legs. They knew I was hanging on by a thread. They saw how much my performance depended on my pain medication. Every move I made, I was being analyzed. I tried to keep the pain from showing up on my face. I kept a neutral expression, but John could read it like a book—like always. He knew exactly what I was doing, how much pain I was in, how hard I was trying to hide it, for myself and for him. People always were analyzing him and watching his every move. If they saw him pushing a gymnast who was showing excruciating pain on her face to compete, it wouldn't be good for him either. My poker face was out of respect for my image and for his.

I have a picture from bars at Regionals that adequately shows the pressure people placed on my shoulders for this meet. Competition was happening everywhere, but there was a crowd that had gathered behind me to watch my bar routine. I started my routine far behind the high bar, and it required me to get close to where they had gathered. I could feel their eyes burning into my back as I saluted. Waiting, wanting to see me fall. They wanted to be front and center to see the top seed fail. They do this in every sport, and it's gross. The number of times my parents sat in front of parents watching me and yelling, "Fall!" to me is sickening. Again, we are viewed as objects and not humans. Not *people* who trained for twenty years for this moment. To them, we were just entertainment, or roadblocks for their own daughters' success. Never humans.

I saluted. Cue words began.

Time went slowly as I swung for my dismount. It always did. Like a movie, the most dramatic moment took the longest to complete. My feet hit the mat and didn't move. Stuck. My eyes looked up to the crowd that had gathered behind where I started and stared for a split second. I turned and saluted to the judges to complete my routine. Two down, two to go.

Beam. The event everyone had seen me fall on the year before. I hadn't fallen since. If there was a place to have hope for my failure, it was here. My competition didn't know I had prepared beam to handle the most stressful pressure sets through my visualizations. I was confident in my training. My belief in the way I had practiced trumped the uncertainty I felt in my legs. I saluted for beam, and my cue words began.

Deep breath before my dismount: "breathe, pose, prepare, hurdle, punch, spot, stick." Kathryn stood directly behind the beam for my dismount to hold my mat for my landing. This also always made her the first person I hugged after I saluted. John watched beam from a distance because it was Kathryn's event, but I could hear his whistle. Three events down, one to go.

I was in first place going into floor, my best event. If I did what I usually did, I would be a Regional Champion. My pain medication had worn completely off, and my legs were entirely numb. I was relying solely on adrenaline for my longest routine. During warm-ups, I could feel the weakness in my legs starting to be difficult to work through. I stood in the corner to warm up my middle pass: a two-and-a-half-punch front. My cue words began: "push, hurdle, handspring, punch, set, pull, spot, punch." My legs crumbled under me. The punch front was so low my hair bun grazed the floor. I landed flat on my back. I could hear the crowd uncontrollably gasp in shock as the leading gymnast showed weakness on her strongest event.

I stood up and walked to another corner. We only had four minutes to warm up three passes, so I had no time to sit and think about why I fell or let the pain from crashing subside. I didn't need time to think about it. I knew the fall was because I had no feeling in my legs. It was completely gone; it felt like I was walking on air. I looked over to John. He knew it wasn't my technique that was wrong. He walked onto the floor to the opposite corner I was facing to warm up my third pass. Without saying anything to each other, he knew I needed him to spot me warming up my last pass. He wasn't going to let me fall again. I began running toward him to warm up my double back. I felt his hand push my back up to give me the height I needed to land safely. I flipped twice in the air and felt his hands grab my arm and back lifting them up so I landed with much less force on my body. He put all of his strength into protecting my body, making sure I didn't fall. He held me up.

I sat down and rubbed more Icy Hot into my legs. I felt nothing. I went to Larry's room. He gave me Biofreeze to layer on top of the Icy Hot. I walked back into the arena. I had three more girls before it was my turn to go, so I sat back down. I looked up at my parents in the crowd. Smile and hand heart. My face stayed neutral. Young girls lined the floor behind the ropes to watch. If the crowd of parents wasn't bad enough, now I had little gymnasts, too, waiting to watch me.

I couldn't let myself fall. Before I knew it, it was my turn. I stood at the edge of the corner waiting for the judge to raise her flag. I saw John at the other edge of the floor. He was waiting by the corner I was going to finish my last pass in. He was there to comfort me. Again, without his saying anything, I knew if something went wrong in the routine he was going to catch me. He would walk onto the floor without hesitation to not let me fall. He would let the judges take a large deduction off my score to protect me. Kathryn came to give me the final words before my routine instead.

"You have got this, Rach. Come on, let's go. Attack this." She lifted both fists and I lifted mine. We high-fived with our knuckles, and I turned to salute the judge.

I positioned myself in my starting pose, and time slowed down. The sounds of the crowd and the arena drowned out. I heard only my breath. It was shaking. My music began, and my body followed. My cue words started. I stood in the corner and took a deep breath before my first pass. I heard John clapping, and I saw him out of the corner of my eye with his straight right hand reminding me to be tight. "Push, hurdle, handspring, set, flip, flip, spot, lunge."

One pass down, two to go.

I heard John whistle. I could feel my anxiety reach new levels as I got closer and closer to my second pass that I hadn't landed in warm-ups. I could feel my legs shaking and tingling. I could feel how hard it was to move my feet. They felt like they were four feet deep in quicksand. I felt myself drift away from my cue words and my head filled with doubt and fear. My choreography turned me around to face the corner for my second pass. John had moved. He stood directly behind this corner. A sense of safety flew through my body. He would be right there if something went wrong. My cue words returned.

"Push, hurdle, handspring, punch, set, pull, spot, punch, spot, land, lunge."

John whistled harder as an enormous smile formed on my face. The crowd of little girls sitting next to the floor cheered. Two down, one to go. I saw John swiftly shift over to the corner of my final pass. I took multiple deep breathes in choreography breaks. I faced the corner for my final pass. I saw John, ready for anything. He was analyzing every movement I made, looking for signs of weakness and hints of what my body needed him to do. His chin was lowered and his eyes were peering above his glasses in focus. My cue words began for the final pass.

"Push, hurdle, handspring, set, flip, flip, spot, lunge."

John's whistle was louder than ever as he walked away from the edge of the floor. He clapped hard as my choreography ended and my music stopped. I smiled uncharacteristically big as I saluted the judge one last time that meet. I had qualified to Nationals one last time as a Regional Champion.

Preparing for my last Nationals was bittersweet. I was excited to be competing in the state I would call my home just a few weeks later, but I was sad to be leaving the place I had made my home for so long. My Minnesota coaches were thrilled about my performance at Regionals and were excited to be the host state for Nationals. They told me a

Rachel Haines, Regionals 2013. *USAG*

few of my future teammates would even be in attendance since it was so close to campus.

I trained like I was going to win Nationals. I wanted so much to win floor. I wanted to make the National team one last time. I wanted to leave my mark for Twistars and get off on the right foot for Minnesota. I felt the pressure to succeed that came with where I was in the national rankings and how my season had been going. I knew I had already made the colleges that turned me down regret their decision, so I had one last chance to make the college that took me proud.

I remember thinking on the flight to Nationals that I would be doing this travel often over the next few years. I started to accept that my road as a club gymnast was coming to an end. I was beginning to imagine and visualize myself as a college gymnast. I was preparing myself for the next chapter.

The arena was huge and beautiful, right in the center of the city. Again, a big curtain separated the warm-up gym from the competition gym. Still hated that thing. During the practice day, I made a point to go and talk to my new coaches. I was allowed to communicate with them now that I had signed my National Letter of Intent. They intimidated the crap out of me. They congratulated me on the season I was having and said they were excited to watch me the following day. They reminded me that some girls on the team would be coming to watch as well since I was competing with a few other Gopher recruits in my session. This stressed me out.

I woke up the morning of competition very emotional. I was sad to be competing for John and Kathryn one last time. I wanted to make them proud. I wanted to represent them the best I could. My mom did my hair with three thousand bobby pins and gave me my ice cream sandwich one last time.

I never ate an ice cream sandwich before a meet after that.

I walked over to the arena with the girls who had qualified with me at Regionals. We were all pretty close. We were often the same girls who qualified together the previous years, and we frequently competed against each other during the regular season. Competing with them was especially fun because of how well we got along. We all had committed to different colleges and would continue to see each other as rivals for the next four years. One was off to Illinois, one was going to Nebraska, one to Ohio State, one to Western Michigan, and one to the Air Force Academy. We were all emotional that we were headed in different directions after this meet, and we fed off each other to make this meet our best one yet.

At the arena, I saw my Minnesota coaches behind their Minnesota nameplate. I smiled and waved and headed behind the curtain to the practice gym. We started to warm up for our first event. We would be on floor first. I had so much energy for this event, and I would have to control it. This was the event I wanted to do the best on. I wanted to go a full season undefeated. I had to control my excitement and power if I wanted the routine to be good.

Mid-warm-up, one of our teammates crashed onto the floor and curled into a ball in the corner. We all stopped tumbling and looked. Our time kept running, but we all cared more about our teammate. She had torn her Achilles on the first event's warm-up and ended her career as a club gymnast. Displaying every parent's worst fear, she emerged from behind the practice gym curtain with her foot in a thick cast and on crutches.

I warmed up on floor and looked into the stands to see my parents. I also saw the Minnesota gymnastics team standing next to the bleachers watching. I saw my Minnesota coaches standing near the floor with an iPad up and ready to record my routine. So many people waiting to watch my routine . . . waiting to judge it. I told myself to stay controlled, to not let my energy launch me so hard that I would end out of bounds.

I was up early in the lineup and didn't have long enough after warm-ups to sit and rest. It all felt so fast because I was trying to make it go as slow as possible. I was trying to embrace every moment left as a club gymnast. Before I knew it, I was raising my hands to salute. Standing in my starting pose, I could feel my heart pump through my leo so hard you could see it. My cue words began. I was already in the first corner, about to do my first pass.

"Push, hurdle, handspring, set, flip, flip, spot, lunge."

I felt the power I had in my legs for the first event. I could feel myself losing control of my adrenaline. I had to control it for the next two passes. I thought about breathing and relaxing for the choreography leading up to my second pass. I was now in corner number two, about to do my two-and-a-half-punch front.

"Push, hurdle, handspring, punch, set, pull, spot, punch, spot, land, lunge."

I landed in the corner closest to the Minnesota gymnasts who had come to watch. They were standing close and were the first thing I saw when my eyes focused after my flip. I felt adrenaline surge through me. My heart thumped harder. I wanted to impress them. I wanted to make sure they knew I was worthy of being their teammate. "Breathe, Rach. Slow down," I told myself as I approached the corner for my last pass.

"Slow, hurdle, soft, handspring, set, flip, flip, spot, lunge."

I held back too much. I changed my cue words, and I paid the price. My chest landed low and my lunge went forward instead of backward. Big deduction. My heart, which had been thumping so hard with excitement, skipped a beat and sunk. I literally felt myself rip the floor title out of my own hands, all because I was too focused on what others were thinking of my gymnastics. All because I altered myself to make others think I was worthy.

I got off the floor pissed, and John could see it. He knew what my goals were. He knew I had blown one of them on the very first event. We walked back behind the curtain to the warm-up gym to warm-up vault. The remainder of the meet was nothing spectacular, and therefore I don't remember the exact details. I do remember finishing my beam routine and crumbling into John and Kathryn's arms, but mostly just because there are pictures of the moment. I was sad to be done with Twistars and moving to new coaches, and you could see it.

I ended up taking fourth that year, three-tenths away from a national title (my deduction on floor). I was behind future Stanford, LSU, and Oregon State gymnasts. I was proud to be the first Big Ten athlete on the podium. (For the record, I took fourth on floor as well; .05 away from the champion's score.)

Rachel Haines and Kathryn Geddert, Nationals 2013. *USAG*

Rachel Haines and John Geddert, Nationals 2013. *USAG*

Looking back, I am upset at myself for letting my fear of what people thought of me change my floor routine. I am more mad that I still do that in all aspects of life. It started in elementary school with the talent show, and it happened at my senior year Nationals. I changed my actions to match what people wanted me to do and what would make them think I was good enough. I have seen it in previous relationships, jobs, and even the way I look. I match my personality with the needs of my surroundings. I am a chameleon in life. Because of that, I have a hard time knowing who Rachel is when she doesn't care about what people think. I don't know who the real me is because I was in a sport that shaped my identity, that made me think I should match who I am to who others wanted me to be.

Otherwise, I wouldn't be good enough.

CHAPTER NINE

~

College

Transitioning from club to college gymnastics is difficult. The changes I went through at eighteen years old were uncountable. When I arrived on campus, I moved into an apartment with the three other freshman gymnasts. It was intimidating to go from living with my parents straight to having my own apartment. I didn't know how to cook, clean a toilet, or do laundry. This may sound crazy, but when I was up from 5:30 a.m. to 11:00 p.m. for school and practice every day, I never had time to learn. I was basically thrown to the wolves to fend for myself.

Practice structure changed a crazy amount. For one, now we lifted weights. I had never lifted before in my life; it just wasn't something club gymnasts did. In club, it is all about body weight lifting, circuits, and toning. Now, we had to be at weights at 5:00 in the morning doing squats and bench presses to bulk up. I got enormous. My shoulders stuck out even more, my arms became Hulk replicas, and my legs looked like they each weighed 100 pounds. This was terrible for my back. My spine was crumbling carrying the 120 pounds I was going into college, and now I was forcing it to carry a lot more muscle everywhere. I felt it get worse and worse because of these lifts.

Practices at the gym changed, too. Now we had the open gym design I had seen as a recruit. I did aerobics for warm-ups instead of running. I got to choose which event I went to, how long I stayed on it, and what I did. Being used to a rigorous club practice, I did way too much for the college standard. I was doing full routines to make sure everyone knew I wasn't a slacker—all of us freshmen were. We didn't know the expectations, and we for sure didn't want to fall below them.

After sixteen years of doing gymnastics one way, the transition to college was that much more difficult. Our equipment, practices, schedule, coaches, team, and home all changed at the same moment. It was a lot to adapt to, and we put a lot of pressure on ourselves to adapt quickly. I was blessed to have the coaches I did at Minnesota. They coached with a different style than John's, which was to be expected since we were closer to adults at this point and should have more maturity than we did in high school. They were patient with us for the time it took us to get used to all of the changes.

When athletes get to campus as freshmen, we are required to see the trainers and doctors at the school to get clearance to do gymnastics. Even though we had already committed, signed the National Letter of Intent, registered for classes, and moved in, the medical team at the university still held the power to say an athlete was too much of a liability to compete at their university. Seems a bit unfair, right?

Some of the girls weren't cleared to do gymnastics for a few weeks after getting on campus due to ankle injuries they suffered their senior season. I was terrified. If they didn't clear ankle injuries, they would definitely not clear a multiple-fractured, shattered back. Seeing the trainer and doctor for clearance didn't start out well. They were extremely skeptical of the stability of my back and questioned my safety continuing the sport after seeing my MRI scans. Just like every doctor I had seen, they discouraged me from continuing the sport. They asked how I was able to come back from an injury like this and compete four events so successfully. I told them who my doctor was at home who nursed me back to being a competitor.

I told them to talk to Larry.

Larry convinced them I was stable. He told them that my back wasn't getting any worse, and as long as I could stand the pain I was able to do the sport. He offered up his suggestions for therapy for me. He sent over sheets upon sheets of rehab exercises. For some reason, he never mentioned his "internal manipulation" to my new therapists as a source of relief.

I wonder why he wanted to keep that a secret.

Because I had been enduring the treatment for four full years, I just figured my new trainers weren't well educated enough to do this type of therapy. Only someone as prestigious and well known as Larry could do it. I now know that if I had just asked my new trainers (two women) if they knew about the treatment, the abuse could have been brought to light a lot sooner. But I trusted Larry with everything. If he didn't want them to continue that part of my "treatment" at Minnesota, I figured there was a reason.

He ended the phone call with my trainers saying that whenever I came home I could continue to see him for therapy as well to ensure my stability in gymnastics.

They believed him, clearing me to do gymnastics at Minnesota. They knew Larry Nassar's name before I told them he was my trainer. They trusted him like I had. He was so well known, his opinion trumped their education. His power and authority trumped their discomfort with letting me continue to do gymnastics. Here Larry was convincing two more doctors of my safety for his own personal pleasure while my legs were getting more numb and discs were sliding further into my spinal cord, causing permanent damage.

It isn't like my back was feeling any better since I broke it, but I was still grateful for Larry's ability to convince my doctors to clear me. I still couldn't sleep flat on my back or on my belly. I could sleep only on my side with a pillow between my legs. I could stand only for ten minutes max, and then I had to sit. But I could sit only for ten minutes before I had to stand again because of the pain. Staying still made the muscles get tense and the pain worse, but it also hurt to move. It hurt to bend down to sit on a toilet. It hurt to tie my shoes and to lift anything heavier than a milk carton. I was in excruciating pain, but not being cleared would have hurt worse.

Preseason is the most difficult time of the year for a college gymnast. It is when assignments are the hardest, conditioning hurts the most, and stress levels are at new highs. It is especially difficult for freshmen. The most challenging time of training is also during our first semester as a college student. And it is the longest time most of us had gone without seeing our parents. We weren't allowed to miss practices to go home, and the first time we would be able to wasn't until Thanksgiving. My anxiety was at an all-time high during preseason my freshman year. I think I called my mom a total of eight times claiming to be dropping out of college.

My back was falling apart in preseason. The lifting that was added to my training in college was starting to show its negative side effects. My legs were dead under me. My back hurt just as much as it did right after I broke it. My big toe was getting harder to lift. The warning signs for lifelong consequences of my injury were becoming more prevalent.

But I still didn't stop, because Larry told me I didn't have to.

Being placed in the lineup for events as a freshman is an honor. I felt excitement surge through my body when I saw that I had been chosen to be in the vault, floor, and beam lineups for the first meet. That summer, the Minnesota coaches required all of the freshmen to adapt to a new bar setting where the low bar was raised and the high bar was lowered. You can't imagine how difficult it is to adapt to a new setting on bars. Every skill has to be relearned, as timing is completely different. I never got used to the setting they required us to use, and therefore I quit training bars forever. I had made the lineups on every event that I trained.

To be honest, freshman year was a blur. I know that I fell in love with competing, as college meets are so much more theatrical than club meets. I remember walking into the Pavilion the day of my first meet as a Golden Gopher. Instead of the normal cluttered arena, like at club meets, there was only one set of each apparatus. It was clean, with maroon and gold everywhere. I remember walking into our own locker room and thinking it was the most amazing thing I could've asked for. We had our own cubby with our name and picture above it, like celebrities. Lining the ledge next to the mirrors were ten pounds of glitter, stick-on tattoos, and ribbons we would decorate ourselves with. We stuck jewels next to our eyes and tattoos of the block "M" on our cheeks. All of us matched exactly, and I felt like I was truly a part of a family.

As our timed stretch warm-up began at the first meet and our opposing team started running in the typical circle, our team's aerobics music started playing and we did our dance routine instead. I thought it was awesome that we did something so unique. We all were laughing at the comical choreography in the routine, and I was feeling less tense about the competition the further along we got through the dance.

I know I only fell once during this season, and it was because my legs were so numb on beam they launched me completely to the side and I bashed my hip into the beam in one gnarly-looking crash. I am not surprised it is my "most viewed" routine on YouTube—it's pretty funny.

We were successful as a team my freshman year. We defeated Air Force, Lindenwood, Washington, New Hampshire, Brown, Yale, Illinois, Ohio State, Michigan State, Iowa State, Winona, Hamlin, Gustavus, Texas Women's, Penn State, Michigan, and Iowa. Team success continued as I transitioned out of Twistars and into Minnesota. I loved winning. I loved watching us climb in the rankings. I enjoyed being on a team more than I had in club. My first meet, I felt the motivation shift from worrying about how I did to worrying about how the team did. I wanted to do well for my team and not only for myself anymore. I know I scored a 9.775 for my very first routine on vault in college. Not super, but it put me in third place for the first meet. I got a 9.7 on my very first beam routine, which put me in second place for the meet as well.

That year, our team would defeat enough Big Ten teams to be crowned the Regular Season Big Ten Champions. This was such an incredible honor to have achieved in my first season with the Gophers. We earned huge, glamorous rings with our names engraved on them. I wore that ring so proudly.

Our team was successful enough that year to also qualify for the Regional Competition. The structure of meets was the same for college gymnastics as it was for club. Do well at Regionals, and we qualify to Nationals. I was so used to expecting to go to Nationals that when everyone was in a frenzy about "How can we qualify?" I didn't understand. I had never *not* made it to Nationals. Not qualifying wasn't an option. I had no idea how insanely difficult it was to make it. The top two teams from Regionals make it to Nationals. In college I had to start thinking about rankings and seedings, because they now had an effect on who our opponents were. For Regionals, we had to beat two teams that were better than we were, as we came in seeded third.

I remember the hype and drama of the meet as all the decorations turned blue for the NCAA. The stands filled with a thousand more fans than usual. It was overwhelming. The pressure was high, and the thrill of competing in that atmosphere was addicting. My visualizations had prepared me for this exact moment. It was obnoxiously loud. I absolutely loved it.

We fought hard at Regionals, and ended up .025 shy of qualifying to Nationals behind a team we had already defeated that year. It was heartbreaking. I didn't know how to cope with a season that didn't end with Nationals. It had never happened to me before. I had a minor identity crisis after my freshman year as I watched my season be controlled by the success of more people than just myself. Being on a team after having been more focused on individual success for eighteen years was extremely challenging.

I knew that the following year I was not going to be okay with not making it to Nationals again.

CHAPTER TEN

Divided

Emotional distress number three.

When gymnasts are in the recruiting stage of their careers, they look for five main things on their campus visits. We're teenagers, remember, so our priorities aren't necessarily in the order they should be. To be honest, academics were nowhere on my priority list. For my friends and me at least, our college searches revolved around focusing on five different characteristics:

1. How successful was the gymnastics team? This was solely based on rankings. I only cared about teams that would continue to put me on the top of the podium because I knew losing wasn't an option for me. I needed a team that would continue to give me opportunities to win.

2. What kind of perks did we get? Selfish and shallow, I know, but it's true. I wanted the fancy gear, I wanted free meals, I wanted a school that showered me with gifts because I was an athlete. I wanted to be on a campus that distinguished the student-athletes from just the students. I wanted blingy athletic gear with backpacks that screamed "gymnast" on them. I wanted my athleticism to be clear, because it was my entire identity.

3. How good were the facilities? I cared a lot about what the gym looked like. I came from Twistars, hands down one of the best

club gymnastics facilities in the nation. My expectations were high. I wanted new beam covers, bouncy floors, and anything but Spieth bars.

4. How fun did the campus look? At sixteen years old, I wanted a campus filled with cute boys and entertaining surroundings. I wanted the loudest football games with the best fast-food restaurants.

5. What were the coaches like? I cared a lot about what the coaches were like when I was in the recruiting process. I wanted coaches who cared about me as a person, pushed me to work harder, understood my injury, and were competitive, classy, and experienced. I wanted coaches who had been there for a long time because that usually meant they weren't going anywhere soon.

I picked a gymnastics program that wasn't in the top ten of the rankings, didn't flood their athletes with as much gear as other schools, trained in a tiny facility that used to be a high school gym, and had a campus that was covered in freezing rain and snow nine months out of the year. It was pretty clear that I sacrificed a lot of what I was looking for because I was so drawn to the coaches at Minnesota.

Never go to a college just because of the coaches.

Shortly after season ended, things started to change. Our male head coach stopped coming to practices. There were rumors and tons of tension on the team. The freshmen were kept entirely in the dark until one day an article was published.

"Gymnastics coach out at U of M after sexual harassment investigations."—*Star Tribune.*

One of my teammates had come forward as a victim of our male coach, and our team was in shock. It seemed the upperclassmen were in on the details long before the news came out. They all knew which teammate it was and what the allegations were. We freshmen, on the other hand, were left completely in the dark. We had no idea what was happening besides the fact that one of our coaches was never going to be returning to practice. His wife, our head coach, remained.

Our team began to self-destruct. Some of the girls took the side of the victim, claiming to have also been made to feel uncomfortable by advances by our coach. Some of us had no idea what was happening. There was a clearly defined line that divided our team into two armies. Our close-knit culture crumbled.

Time kept moving and we kept practicing. The gym had the largest elephant in the room as we tried to work past the larger issue none of us wanted to talk about. The victim wouldn't admit it was her to the underclassmen, and it made us resent those who were older. Seniority trumped fairness and equality. We knew that everyone else except us knew what was going on, and it stung. Our team lost every connection we had built the previous year.

A few months later, we were hit with another brick in the face.

The highly successful coach of the University of Minnesota women's gymnastics team resigned Thursday after a year of claims of sexual harassment and retaliation within the team. The school determined that [our head coach], one-time national coach of the year, retaliated against someone at the university after a student-athlete claimed she was sexually harassed by [her] husband.—*Star Tribune*

Our head coach was gone. Investigation after investigation happened that summer. I was interviewed so many times about things I knew nothing about. I had no information, yet my coach's job depended on the answers I gave. Because I was kept in the dark by the upperclassmen, I was watching my program crumble before my eyes in my second year there, with no understanding as to why.

Our team fell apart. Half of us resented the other half because they weren't telling us the truth. The other half resented us because we weren't being empathetic in a situation we knew nothing about. We went into the search for a new head coach with a clearly cold culture. The team interviewed three coaches for the open position: two outside applicants, and one in-house applicant. The assistant coach we had the year before decided to apply and had made it to the final round of interviews.

This wreaked havoc on the team.

For one, the male assistant coach had also applied for the position. He failed to make it to the end of the interview process and made his anger clear. He claimed racial discrimination was the cause of his failure to make it to the final round, and we all entered into yet another round of investigations and interviews I had no idea about. The tension in the gym was unmistakable as the team was split into two resentful sides, and the two remaining coaches despised each other, splitting up our staff as well.

Practice was hell. Not because of the difficulty or demands of the practice, but because of the stress that had been added to our team.

My anxiety and panic reached an even higher level as I questioned my decision to attend the University of Minnesota. As a freshman, I was already regretting where I had chosen to be. I had never been in such a toxic and spiteful atmosphere, and it was ruining my passion for the sport. Our team was getting so much negative attention that we could barely keep our culture presentable in the dark let alone with a spotlight beaming onto it.

It was clear the underclassmen demanded some sort of consistency. We wanted the coaching position to be filled by someone we knew and trusted because we felt like everything in our lives was changing. We had already gone through the biggest transition of our lives that year, and now what we thought would remain constant for at least four years was changing, too. We wanted the head coach to be our current assistant coach, and half of the team voiced their disapproval. Again we were disagreeing on something both sides were passionate about, and nobody was going to budge on their opinions.

It was clear that the close culture that had been advertised to me as a top priority on my recruiting trip was not something that I would experience. It became obvious that what I had been promised, I was not going to get.

Our assistant coach was named as interim head coach in October. This was midway through preseason, when we were supposed to be perfecting the smallest deductions in our routine, not finally solidifying who would coach us. Our male assistant coach left, and we remained with two open coaching positions. Those spots would officially be filled in December, one month before the season began. We went into the season unprepared, divided, and broken.

That year we defeated Iowa State, Michigan State, Ohio State, New Hampshire, Iowa, Maryland, and Rutgers. We went from a 27–6 record the year before to a 12–16 record. The reason our win number was even that high was because we faced teams we could beat multiple times in the same season. We were nowhere close to qualifying to Nationals for the second year. My pride in my gymnastics, and my team, was damaged. We were distant and disconnected as a team, and you could see it. We had lost our culture, and everyone could tell. Our success as gymnasts reflected our success as a team.

I had begun to break down mentally, physically, and emotionally.

My back pain reached a new level. It was becoming unbearable and made me resent going to practices. During the summer of 2015, I reached out to Larry for advice. I told him how much it hurt, and how I was forced to stop training floor because it hurt so much. My favorite event was taken from me because of my stupid injury. I cried on the phone with him. He knew I was calling for reassurance that I was okay; he knew I wanted him to say he believed in me; he knew I was calling him as my one last hope of continuing my career.

"I think it is time for you to be done. Gymnastics isn't safe for you to do anymore."

My world came to a stinging halt. What . . . what did he just say? Did Larry just tell me I was done? My chest burned red, my muscles started to twitch in seizurelike movements. My head clouded. My breathing turned into hyperventilating. The only man who ever believed in me didn't anymore. The only doctor who told me my comeback was possible said it no longer was. The only person who had ever given me hope took it away. He was so cold, like he had never cared. My mind was spinning. Everything I thought I knew, I questioned. Everything was fuzzy, except for the one obvious thing that was slapping me in the face.

If Larry thought I should be done, then I should be done.

I knew Larry rarely told people their bodies weren't able to do gymnastics anymore. Why would he? It would lessen his pool of victims. I knew when he suggested quitting, you quit. It was the last resort for Larry. His wildcard statement. If he played his wildcard, you knew you had reached the end of the deck.

I thought more often than I can describe about why Larry changed his mind at this moment.

What was different then from all the times I had wanted his opinion before? Why did he stop fighting for me?

I have since figured out why. Larry was faced with a misconduct complaint in 2014, the very beginning of the storm. He was not charged, but in 2015, right when Larry told me my career was over, he was fired from USA Gymnastics for sexual misconduct. The claims were increasing. Victims were coming forward. He was getting scared.

Larry knew what storm was coming. He knew exactly what was going to happen to him because of the number of gymnasts he abused. He knew I was one of his victims, a regular and consistent victim. He cut me loose so

I would stop seeing him. He hoped I would forget the "treatment" he had performed on me for six years. He tried to disconnect from everyone he had abused in the hope the storm would dissipate instead of continuing to grow.

Little did he know that the storm would grow to be more terrifying than his worst nightmare.

~

CHAPTER ELEVEN

Last One, Best One

One month before Larry told me to quit, I posted to the Facebook world how I felt about having two years left.

Today marks the official beginning of preseason for NCAA Women's Gymnastics. It marks the beginning of the 19th year of my gymnastics career. And also, it marks the beginning of my last two years of the sport I've known my whole life. Some may understand the demand of my sport, but for those who don't, here's just my personal example. 5 years ago I suffered two back fractures leading to the recognition of two bulging discs into my spinal nerves, two degenerative discs, spondylolisthesis, nerve damage causing significant numbness throughout my legs, and arthritis pain on top of those broken bones. For 5 years I've spent countless hours at doctors offices, physical therapy, and doing rehab just to do this crazy sport I love. I've retired an event I enjoyed, sacrificed numbers during practices, used up over 100 icy hot tubes, and experienced 7 back procedures. For those who know just my challenge, you think I'm crazy. For those who know the sport firsthand, you understand why I'm relentless.

So this year, with 19 down and 2 to go, I'm not going to tell you the goals I have for this final homestretch.

I'm going to show you.

I am going to be honest, I think part of me posted this because I wanted to give people a reason as to why I wasn't as stellar in college as I was in club. I wanted to remind them of my injury so I had an excuse.

Another part of me wanted to document my feelings and my goals. If they were documented, then I had to reach them. If I told the world I was going to show them my aspirations over the next two years, then I had to train like it. I was fueling my own fire.

Larry took away my time.

By telling me to quit, he had obliterated my dreams, and with them, my happiness. Here I fell deeper into a hole of depression than I had ever been. Nobody was fighting for me anymore. Nobody believed in me. I met nobody's expectations. All of my deepest, darkest fears hit me at once. I entered into a black hole of identity crisis as the only thing I knew was being ripped away from me.

I am not done with gymnastics.

I can't be.

I didn't know how to be anything but a gymnast. At this point, my anxiety attacks should have placed me in a hospital. Everything set me off. My body would burn, my chest went from turning red to breaking out in hives, I would hyperventilate until my face tingled numb, my eyes would get to the point of tunnel vision, and I shook uncontrollably. I looked like I was having seizures. My anxiety attacks have never been anything less than this traumatizing since Larry told me to quit in 2015.

I talked to my coaches and my trainers about my options. My parents had said whatever I decided to do they supported me, but they made it clear that if I chose to continue the sport I would be putting myself in great danger. I knew they were worried, but they knew there were consequences to both options. If I quit, I would drop into an unhealthy and terrifying level of depression. If I continued, my body would continue to put me in extreme danger. It was truly a lose-lose decision.

I wasn't done. I didn't want to be. I wanted more time.

My coaches and trainer gave me one year. They told me I could compete for one more season, but then I had to be done. They thought this worked out perfectly, as I had enough credits to graduate this year too. It would truthfully be my senior season. They made it clear that I would barely practice and that my numbers would decrease exponentially. I would no longer be allowed to do any workouts outside of practice. No lifting, no pool workouts, no yoga. I would only train gymnastics. I would continue to get the epidural procedures I was getting done, but more frequently. I would not participate in the preseason. I would do the absolute bare minimum and rely almost entirely on mental preparations.

Again, I was broken.

Again, I was crippled.

Again, I was unworthy.

I sat and watched as my teammates trained for the season and I did rehab. I flashed back to my feelings when I was recovering from the initial fractures years ago. I didn't mind as much this time. I knew my gymnastics career had a death sentence approaching and my days were numbered, so I appreciated every moment I could still call myself a gymnast. I was embracing everything.

I didn't post any formal announcement about my new scenario with gymnastics anywhere. I didn't know how. If I posted it, it would mean I was accepting it, and I was extremely far away from accepting it at that point. I kept silent, and I confused everyone with a caption I posted after our first intersquad meet that year.

"Last one, best one," I wrote.

I got so many texts from friends asking if it was a typo. No, it wasn't. Explaining why I was retiring after this year made me feel like a celebrity leaving a TV show. I felt like I was one of the characters who died on *Grey's Anatomy*. In some ways, part of me was dying. I felt like people always knew me because of my gymnastics. Ever since my kindergarten talent show I was known as "the gymnast." People had a hard time accepting that it was ending and were almost in disbelief. A lot of them understood. If they were from my high school, they remembered my turtle shell of a brace. If they were from my club gym, they remembered my crash. They all knew my injury was terrible but had always seen me as someone who fought through it. It had never gotten in the way of my continuing the sport. They weren't shocked because my career was ending; they were shocked because I was giving up.

My final season as a gymnast I never scored less than a 9.700. By my final year I was doing only beam and vault, and my scores counted for the team score every single time. (Only five of the six scores on each event count; the lowest score is dropped.) But my individual success wasn't what stood out to me my senior season; I was proud of what my team accomplished.

The upperclassmen who had been so separate from us had graduated, and it was almost a working team again. We still had remembrances of damage but were clearly in a healing stage. Our culture began to rebuild. Our coaches strived to encourage team bonding and created numerous opportunities for us to build friendships outside of the gym. We focused on trust, respect, and honesty. No more secrets, and no more cliques.

Our healing showed in our performances. We won our season opener against Iowa State. The following weekend, we dominated our first Big Ten team by knocking down Maryland. We would go on to win our second Big Ten battle against Michigan State University and chalked up another win against Ohio State a week later. We continued to dominate the Big Ten by defeating Illinois. We usually lost to Nebraska, but one week later we knocked them off the podium as well. We remained undefeated as we placed first against Iowa State, Air Force, Hamlin, Winona State, and Gustavus. We crushed my senior night to remain undefeated after nine meets against numerous opponents.

The following weekend we headed to Denver for a double meet weekend against the same two teams on Friday and again on Sunday. Two extremely tough matchups in one weekend. Denver was ranked above us, but we were unstoppable. The excitement we built up for this opponent was contagious. We knew we were capable of anything this year. I remember this meet clearly. The arena was dark and the stands were filled with hundreds of fans. Everyone knew this would be a good meet.

We started on bars. I was no longer a competitor on bars, so I sat and watched so my legs had feeling for vault on the next rotation. I had no control over what happened on floor and bars, and I hated it.

I hated sitting there as I watched my teammates fall one after another on bars against Denver.

On the first event, we had to count a falling score. We had dug ourselves a hole that would require a lot of fighting to get back out of. We either needed a miracle to happen to our routine scores, or we needed Denver to make the same mistake that we did. But Denver wasn't going to make any mistakes. Our team rallied together and faced the challenge ahead with drive and support for each other. We ended the meet having the best vault and beam scores of the season, but fell to Denver by .7 points.

We were so excited to face them again on Sunday for a rematch.

My back couldn't handle double meet weekends, so I wouldn't be competing beam for our second matchup against Denver. I knew if I competed I would fall, and winning as a team was more important than my pride to compete individually. We would be at Air Force for the second meet, a team that was also at the meet on Friday. The competition gym was quaint and clean. I felt the beam just out of habit, even though I wouldn't be competing. It was *super* slippery. Praise Jesus I wasn't competing, because I for sure would have fallen. Part of me was honestly relieved I wouldn't have to try flipping on a beam with a puddle on it.

We started the meet on beam. The girls didn't let the texture of the beam affect their gymnastics at all. They all crushed it, and our excitement moving into vault was contagious to the fans in the crowd. I completed vault, and it was nothing shockingly amazing; probably just my consistently average 9.800. The team score was staying close with Denver for the entire meet. After floor, going into bars, we were leading by just a few tenths. We ended on the event we had fallen apart on two days before. I could feel the hope that Denver had in our repeated failure.

But we thrived on the pressure.

That meet was one of my absolute favorite meets of my lifetime. The happiness we all felt when we beat Denver by breaking a 197.00 team score was immeasurable. Our coaches had said earlier in the year if we broke a 197 they would get us doughnuts, and they kept their word. The love we all had for the sport was radiating through all of us. We knew our potential as a team this year could get us a spot at Nationals, and that is all we wanted.

We repeated our success from my freshman year and again were crowned the Regular Season Big Ten Champions. Again we got enormous and glamorous rings, and again I wore my ring with pride.

That year, Minnesota hosted the Regional Competition. For those who don't know, the top thirty-six teams after the regular season advance to Regionals. Regionals are seeded to prevent two top teams from being at the same Regional, as only the top two teams from Regionals advance to Nationals. When the teams that were coming to Minnesota for our Regionals were announced, we were named as the third seed and would have to fight for that second spot to go to Nationals. When they announced who was coming we knew we had a chance.

Top Seed: Florida
Second: Denver
Third: Minnesota
Fourth: Mizzou
Fifth: BYU

We had beaten Denver that year, but they had also beat us. We knew it was going to be a fight until the end and that every tenth would matter. We trained for Regionals knowing that the slightest deduction could end our season. Since it was my last season, I was fighting with everything I had left to make sure I had two more meets in my career.

It was starting to hit me as I trained for Regionals that the end was near. Sure, I had been preparing for it all year, but when it's right in your face you start to actually feel it. I knew my days left as a gymnast were in the single digits. There is no easy way to describe how an athlete in any sport feels when their sport is coming to an end. You feel the hole in your life starting to form before the sport is even gone. You feel the anxiety and pressure to have a clearly defined plan about what you're going to do when the sport is done. You feel the stress of not knowing what to do, since nobody will be telling you what to do anymore.

You feel lost.

You can't find your mom in the grocery store kind of lost.

You lost service on Maps in the middle of nowhere kind of lost.

It is a terrifying thing to reach the line where knowledge ends and the unknown begins. You cross that line when you come to the end of your athletic career. I was inching closer and closer to the line I had been trying to avoid for six years, the line Larry helped me avoid for six years. Everything that I knew and was comfortable with was coming to an end. My talents were only in gymnastics, and it was being taken away from me.

I felt like I was being forced to sing at my elementary school talent show.

Practices were opportunities for me to drain every last ounce of passion I had for the sport. Walking into Regionals was my opportunity to leave everything on the floor. I was not going to hold anything back. I watched as the other teams walked into the Pavilion and started to tour around the equipment. I saw Denver walk in. Both teams knew that it was going to be either us or them who made it to Nationals. It would depend on who decided to show up that day.

We started the meet on floor, an event I didn't contribute on. I sat and watched, cheering my heart out as the Gophers, one by one, nailed their routines. We had set ourselves up with a solid start. We scored a 48.900 as a team for floor before moving onto vault.

I had an opportunity to make an impact on vault. I was third in the lineup and watched as my teammates before me did their job putting up scores. I stood on the runway for my turn, just staring at the vault. My mind started to think about the reality of this meet.

"This could be your last vault. You get one more in your entire lifetime."

My eyes watered then, and they water as I remember it now. I really can't describe the pain I felt realizing that it could be my last time saluting for vault. It tore me to pieces. My arms lowered after my salute to the judges and I refocused onto the vault table.

Deep breath, and my cue words began. A new desire to succeed propelled my legs forward. My last vault would be a great one.

"Push, harder, hurdle, roundoff, block, tight, spot, stick."

My feet rebounded off of the mat with power, and I ended with a slight hop backward. 9.800. My eyes watered as I ran back down the runway toward my team. If that was it, I had accepted it. I took off my wrist guards, and instead of throwing them sloppily into my bag like usual, I took all of the Velcro straps and wrapped them straight and tight around each brace so they were folded nicely, the way they came. I placed them back into their plastic bag, where they hadn't been since the day I had gotten them two years before.

Subconsciously, I was closing this chapter of my life.

Bars was a blur; all I could think about was beam. We were fighting right alongside Denver, but Mizzou was also placing in the running for a top-two spot. Everyone had shown up to fight that day. I knew it would come down to beam. I was fourth in the lineup for beam, with one senior in front of me and the two other seniors behind me. All of us could be closing our final meet together, one after another. It was truly set up to be an emotional and dramatic ending.

We walked over to beam as time was counting down before our touch warm-ups would begin.

Two minutes left.

I paced next to the beam. I stretched out my shoulders and took deep breaths. I warmed up my skills on the line on the floor next to the beam. I turned and looked into the crowd to find my parents. I gave them a look that said, "Here we go, Mom and Dad, one last time." My eyebrows relaxed and I gave them a small closed-mouth smile. My shoulders raised and my eyes watered. They knew. My mom smiled, and my dad shaped a heart. I turned back around to face the beam before tears started to fall. I didn't want to be done. I didn't want this to be my last routine. I wasn't ready.

One minute left.

I walked over to the pile of chalk and wiped it on my feet and hands. My team organized into our order for warm-ups.

Thirty seconds left.

I walked to my side of the beam. I slapped my legs for feeling.

Ten seconds left.

I closed my eyes. I took a deep breath in and held it. The sound of the buzzer to begin warm-ups rang. Our first teammate mounted the beam and started our touches.

Those four minutes flew by. My muscle memory took over my gymnastics while my mind absorbed every moment. Before I knew it we were huddled in our beam team group with our beam coach for our final pump-up words. I don't remember them. I remember shaking, sweating, and feeling my throat close as waterfalls of tears waited to pour out of my eyes. This was it. I remember analyzing every moment and thinking it was the last.

"This is my last group huddle."

"This is my last time pacing behind the corral."

"This is my last time putting chalk on my feet."

"This is my last time standing by the beam."

Wait—how was it already my turn? My mind had been so distracted thinking about every individual moment that I hadn't paid attention to the routines in front of mine. I was already up. My body shook with nerves; my legs quivered as they fought for feeling. I looked up at the Jumbotron at scores. 9.65, 9.725, 9.775. The scores weren't big enough to qualify to Nationals. John's words flooded back into my head.

"In order to win, we need you to hit."

This was it. This was the moment I had been training for. All of John's final motivational words, all of my visualizations were coming true. My shoulders felt the weight, but my mind was a veteran to pressure sets. I stood next to the beam. My beam coach came up to me to give my final corrections. She could see my nerves taking over my body. She knew the feeling; she had once been a college gymnast too. She said three sentences.

"You are strong. You are calm. You are confident."

Our fists came together like they did before every routine. I turned to face the beam. The judge's flag raised, and my arms followed. I

Rachel Haines and Geralen Stack-Eaton Stenger,
NCAA Regionals 2016. *GopherSports*

looked at the beam, and my hands hovered above it to mount. They were shaking. I took one final deep breath, and my feet left the ground to begin my routine.

My cue words took over my mind to replace the "last time" statements. My routine was flowing forward as one by one I hit my skills. Everything was matching my words, following my counts. My feet were glued to the beam after every skill. After my series finished without a wobble I felt a smile take over my face. My arms raised to begin my dismount. My cue words faded into the background of my thoughts.

"Finish strong," was all I said.

I felt my body flip into the air and my eyes looked to spot the ground for the landing. Slow motion. Dramatic finish. My feet pressed into the mat and didn't move. The air felt cold around me as I heard my team burst into celebration and the Minnesota cheer section stand with excitement.

Rachel Haines, NCAA Regionals 2016. *GopherSports*

Stuck.

My arms slowly raised over my head to salute the judges. My back arched far back to resemble the stereotypical "college salute." My movements were slow, absorbing every moment. I took in every sound, every smell, every feeling of that moment. If it was going to be my last, I was going to remember it. The wall that had been holding my tears back for the entire meet collapsed. I ran back to my team with streams of water falling down my face and raw emotions flowing throughout my body. My muscles were tense, I was yelling. I could feel myself getting farther away from the beam, farther away from gymnastics. I accepted that that routine was my last.

But as I watched my last two teammates compete, I realized that it wasn't.

I watched as our scores were added up, and our name landed in the second-place spot. *No way.* Our team was a clump of screams. We clustered together, bouncing up and down and shrieking. We had made it to Nationals. Our season wasn't over. We had one more meet.

I had two more routines in my gymnastics career.

CHAPTER TWELVE

~

NCAAs

NCAA Nationals is the most amazing competition a gymnast can qualify for besides the Olympics. The best gymnasts in the nation come together for the most dramatic and entertaining battle. The arena is always huge and beautiful and the equipment is always raised on a podium resembling the Olympics. The atmosphere is overwhelmingly thrilling. The stands fill with thousands and thousands of fans all sporting their team's gear in overdramatic fashion. Only the top twelve teams in the nation appear at Nationals, and the hype before it is something I can't begin to describe.

Walking into that arena knowing that I was a qualifier and had the opportunity to compete on that enormous stage gave me chills. I was so happy my career would be ending here. I got to close my enormous chapter on the biggest stage in USA Gymnastics. It was everything I wanted. All of the free gear, the nice hotel, the extra-sparkly leos, the Nationals-specific attire we got from Minnesota; the fancy banquet the night before the meet; and the constant coverage of numerous media even on the practice day made us feel like celebrities. I was going out with a bang no matter how I did simply because of the stage I was performing on.

Every single college gymnast who qualifies to Nationals has one goal in mind: to become an All-American. Being an All-American is almost as prestigious as being a National Champion. The top eight gymnasts on each event get the honorary title. I had only two opportunities to place in the top eight, and I was going to pour my heart into the performances of both of them. If I ended my career as an All-American, all of my goals as a gymnast would be met.

I put a disgusting amount pressure on myself.

I still *put a disgusting amount of pressure on myself.*

I wasn't a standout gymnast in college. I won a few event titles here and there but didn't break any individual school records or get any perfect 10s. I got close, but was never as successful as I was in club. Like I said, I think I peaked senior year. The expectation to become an All-American at Nationals was honestly unrealistic for me. But walking into that arena on competition day, that is what I had my mind set on.

We started on floor, just like we had for Regionals. It almost felt lucky. I got to get out some of the adrenaline that had built up by cheering ridiculously loudly for my teammates. We got to start the meet off with an event that always put up a good score. We performed well enough to catch the eyes of the announcers and opposing teams on floor. Our name was in the hat, as we were scoring just as well as the top schools in the nation. We made everyone know we deserved to be there and it wasn't some sort of fluke of qualification. We moved onto vault with a growing excitement from our fans.

It was my turn to do my job.

I climbed the stairs onto the podium vault to begin warm-ups. I was breathing in every moment. I knew our chances of placing top six and moving on to Super Six the next day were slim, but after what we had done at Regionals I can't even lie: I had a little bit of hope. Standing on the raised runway was indescribable. The stands were loud and obnoxious. Cheering was blasting into my ears from every direction. I swear the runway was moving from the sound vibrations. I thought to myself, "Man, this will suck on beam."

Before I competed, I saw my sister move from the fan section to a section close to the vault. She moved all the way down to the front row and had her phone ready to record. She was always so good at capturing moments for me. She knew how much I appreciated recordings of my meets. Her movement closer to the vault comforted me.

My body had begun to shake from nerves. I watched as my teammates competed in front of me, continuing the momentum we had built on floor. We were still keeping up with the other teams as I climbed the stairs onto the runway for my turn. The noise all faded even before I got to my starting spot. All I could hear was my breath and the sound of my feet on the runway. It was like a movie. Everything was in slow motion. My eyes looked up to the vault and my heart skipped a beat. Again my thoughts went to a "last time" mind-set. This could be my last vault.

My coach approached me for her final words of encouragement. I don't remember what she said. I couldn't even hear her. I tried to listen, but my adrenaline drowned out all sounds. She walked away, and I bent down to put chalk on my feet and slap my legs for feeling. I kept my eyes on the ground, knowing the judge was waiting for me to look at her, and took one final deep breath. My eyes closed, and my head raised. When I opened them, the judge's flag was raised high above her head, signaling me to start. My arms raised to salute, and I stepped onto the vault runway.

My cue words began.

I heard only the sounds of my feet hitting the runway as I ran in slow motion toward the vault. I heard my breath as I lunged toward the springboard for my roundoff. I heard my hands block off the vault table and the wind fly past my ears as I flipped. I heard my feet hit the mat. My feet rebounded slightly backward, but I was a great distance from the horse. It must've been a high vault. I sprinted back to my teammates faster than I had run down the runway. I was clapping and screaming.

9.825.

Not high enough to be named an All-American, and I knew that (I placed seventeenth). I needed at least a 9.9 to hope for a top eight spot. I was happy I still had beam. Our team held onto our chances of keeping up with the big dogs as we headed to bars. I got to use another rotation to calm my nerves before finishing on beam. I stood in the corral and watched my teammates begin to compete. Our energy was high and contagious. We weren't out of the qualifying race halfway through the meet. My hopes were getting higher by the minute. Maybe these weren't my last routines; maybe we would qualify to one more day.

But God had a different plan.

I watched as teammate after teammate fell off the bars. Once the second teammate had fallen, we knew our chances of one more day were unreachable. When the third teammate fell, we entered into a state of embarrassment. The media noticeably stopped paying attention to us as we fell off the radar. You could feel our team's and our fans' energy shift dramatically. Everyone knew our historic season was coming to an end within the next hour. The seniors realized that our careers were ending in one more event.

There was no longer any hope in me. I began to prepare to compete one final time.

I had been through these emotions before at Regionals, but somehow they hit harder. I had started with so much hope, holding onto the possibilities. Reality hit me like a brick. We walked over to beam and I climbed up the stairs onto the beam's podium. I ran my hands along the surface of the beam and my eyes started to water.

Our seniors were accepting reality, and you could feel it. We all looked sad, and the energy had been drained from our team after bars. Our warm-up was almost silent. I watched as my sister crossed the arena to sit closer to beam to record my final routine. I looked up at her, and my eyes watered more.

The world stopped spinning when I walked up the stairs and faced the judges for my final routine. I kept my chin to the ground. My coach came over to me for the final words. I looked up at her.

"You are strong. You are calm. You are confident."

She took a deep breath as she raised her knuckles to mine. She walked away from me to stand behind the beam for my routine.

The judge's flag raised slowly, and my arms followed. I turned to face the beam. I looked down at it, and felt one tear slip past the wall I had built up holding them back. I took an extra deep breath to stop the rest from following. Time stood still. I didn't want to start my routine. I didn't want to start the end. I never wanted to finish this routine.

My feet left the ground, and my cue words began.

My legs shook with nerves as they fought for feeling. I felt my chin quivering as I tried to hold back the tears. My body kept going through the motions of the routine as my cue words played in the background of my thoughts. I kept having to tell myself to take deep breaths to relax. Deep breath before every skill. I felt my body stay even above the beam, perfectly balanced through every skill. Everything was staying in alignment and I wasn't wobbling. Skill after skill, I was nailing my routine. Only my dismount was left. I felt my arms finish the choreography and raise to begin my dismount. I paused extra long.

My last skill as a gymnast.

I felt my body flow forward onto the beam, my hands touched the surface and my leg swooped through for the gainer full. My eyes shifted to spot the ground, and I felt my feet sink into the mat. They rooted themselves into the ground and didn't move.

Stuck.

The tears started falling before my arms raised to salute for the final time. I looked at the judges and it seemed like I had opened my eyes underwater. I ran off the podium, clapping once in celebration of hitting my final routine of my lifetime. My hand covered my mouth as I reached my team. My teammates hugged me and had water in their eyes, too, as they watched all of us seniors take our final bow with gymnastics. Other teams may have been celebrating qualifying to Super Six, but our team by far had the most emotion at the completion of the meet. All of the seniors dismounted the beam with tears in their eyes as we concluded our careers.

My score flashed on the screens. 9.850. That wasn't high enough. I hadn't moved, so why wasn't it above a 9.9? I resented the ambiguity of gymnastics scoring. Looking up at the standings, I was in the top eight at the conclusion of session one. We still had an entire session to get through before I knew if I would finish in the top eight, but there was nothing I could do anymore.

I sat through the second session and watched myself lose the All-American title as gymnast after gymnast scored above me.

I had the seventh highest score of the meet, but because of multiple ties at multiple scores, I ended up thirteenth in the nation, six spots away from reaching my ultimate goal.

I ended my gymnastics career in the top twenty in the nation on both events I competed on the biggest stage for NCAA gymnastics, but it wasn't good enough for me.

CHAPTER THIRTEEN

~

Retirement

I'll try to explain what it feels like to be done with gymnastics. At first, it's a little refreshing. It's almost a honeymoon stage of separation. You're excited to give your body time to finally heal. It's relieving to know that the following week you don't have to be back in the gym pushing through massive amounts of pain. You're future-focused, but only about some things. You try to plan trips and vacations because you know you no longer have practices you have to make. You plan how you're going to fill all of the free time you now have. At first you eat, a lot. I ate massive amounts of junk food, knowing I would never have to cram my body into a leotard in front of hundreds of people again.

But a few weeks later, it hits you.

It hits you when you start getting bored having so much free time. You go from dedicating forty hours a week to a sport to nothing at all. The boredom is overwhelming. Ninety-nine percent of retired gymnasts find their way back into the gym at some point just because it feels like that is where they are supposed to be. It feels weird having nobody tell you what to do. You go from twenty-two years of having what you eat, how much you sleep, what you do, and when you do it decided for you to having no direction at all. You feel lost again.

A few weeks later you start to realize the reality of retirement.

To be honest, the reality of retirement is still haunting me. Gymnastics consumes you. It is your entire world, your life, and your identity, and then it is just taken away from you. People knew me because I was a gymnast, and now I felt like I was nothing. Somehow gymnastics finds a way to make you feel worthless even after you're done with it.

I can't tell you the number of times I have cried because people who have entered my life after I retired never got to see me do gymnastics. I feel like they don't know who I am because they didn't see me do the sport that made me into who I am. They don't know about my accomplishments, my talent, or my injury. They are missing huge pieces to the puzzle of my life and it skews the final picture. They don't know how strong I am. They don't understand how hard I trained. They didn't see me persevere through every obstacle and hurdle gymnastics put me through. They only hear the stories of what I have done. They see only the remnants of a once-talented gymnast.

I can't tell you the number of times I have wanted to make a comeback to show those who have recently entered my life that I am valuable, that I am special. Gymnastics groomed me to think that I was special, that I always had to be. I always have to stand out. I had to at my elementary talent show, and I still do now. I have to prove my worth, and the only way that I know how to do that is through gymnastics. I have been to countless numbers of open gyms and played on the equipment to show those I love that I am worthy of their attention, that I have something unique to offer. Although I no longer wear the numbers on the back of my leotard, I am still trying to sell myself like a state-fair animal.

I am no longer in shape. I am no longer flexible. I am no longer talented. I feel like I am no longer important. I have watched my body change and adapt to not working out forty hours a week. I have watched my mental health and confidence slowly descend to dangerous levels. I can't look in a mirror and not compare myself to what I looked like when I was a gymnast. I hated my body when I was a gymnast, so imagine how I feel about it now. I try to do splits and nearly tear my hamstrings through force because I am embarrassed to not be all the way down. I pinch the skin of my belly, and although it is far from chubby, it is nowhere near the six-pack abs I used to have. My expectations for my body are unrealistic. My perception of a good body image is no longer reachable. The lack of confidence I have in my skin is disgusting.

I find myself reaching and latching onto any opportunity I have to do gymnastics even still. I am now an acrobatics coach at a dance studio. Sometimes I demonstrate flips for them, and I can feel their shock and awe. I still do cartwheels and handstands in my living room. Somehow, it is still showing up in my life.

The first few months after I was done with gymnastics were spent adjusting. It was the biggest transition I had ever gone through in my life. It didn't help that I also graduated college, totaled my car, moved out of the apartment I had been in for two years, and got a new job. Literally every single aspect of my life changed within months. I truly felt like I didn't know who I was because nothing remained constant. I went from college gymnast to unathletic adult.

If that wasn't hard enough, something bigger than I could have imagined or ever prepared for was about to change.

CHAPTER FOURTEEN

Numb

On September 12, 2016, four months after my gymnastics career ended, my world came crashing down. Not even my worst nightmare compared to the news I was reading at my fingertips. Articles, posts, breaking news hits, tweets, shares, and videos flooded my phone.

Dazed, I read, "Larry Nassar, Sexual Assailant."

My mind was rushing but staying silent all the same. My body felt nothing but excruciating pain all at once. My anxiety took over my body. For the first time that I can remember, I was truly speechless.

Numb. Emotionless. Unable to conjure up a single thought.

I called my mom. She asked if I believed the allegations. I had flashbacks of him manipulating me, flashbacks that took over my entire being. I was reimagining his hands performing his "treatments" on me, recalling the very thing I had hoped to leave in my past forever.

I felt his bare, ungloved hands violating me.

I felt the way my body cringed in discomfort. I felt my back sweating, the cold sweat I used to produce every time I had the displeasure of seeing him. In just moments, every uncomfortable, terrible thing Larry Nassar did to me came rushing back. I was reliving it. I was being haunted by Larry Nassar.

"No, they're not true. Or at least not for me," I answered her impulsively. Part of me honestly wasn't able to tell the person who had done everything in her power to keep me safe and protected the true atrocities that Larry's "treatments" involved.

My body trembled the same way it did every moment I was with Larry, but I still didn't believe that it was sexual assault.

Larry was a miracle worker. Nobody should be able to bounce back from three spine fractures and compete at the collegiate level with an otherwise career-ending injury. But Larry had helped me do it. He was a selfless and giving person. He had built a foundation for his daughter to raise awareness for autism. He was working with my dad as a volunteer to develop a surgery that would address back injuries like mine. He had given up his time to be at my beck and call whenever I needed him. This man was not a monster; he was always doing what was best for me. I believed in his "treatments." And I believed in him.

Denial.

My friends and acquaintances declared their opinions on social media. There was a clear divide. There were those who knew he had ulterior motives and those who called "bullshit."

I thought about my sophomore year of college. The divide caused by sexual assault allegations were back to haunt me again.

I avoided declaring my opinion because I was honestly torn. I knew what he did made me uncomfortable, but it was a medical treatment. He had told me it was. In my head, it had worked. There was a correlation. He kept me in all four events of gymnastics for three years while he was treating me. Then I went to college, the "treatments" stopped, and I no longer trained floor or bars.

Even though I was on Larry's side up until this point, I didn't like what I was seeing all over my newsfeed. People were victim shaming right in front of my eyes. They were victim shaming my closest friends. It hurt me more than it did when I fractured my back in three different places.

As time passed, more descriptions of the assaults surfaced. More victims came forward—more of my friends. I remember sitting in my apartment, laying in bed, scrolling through one of the first statements released by one of the victims. She began to describe her "treatments" from Larry in great detail, and I could feel my heart stop beating for a few seconds.

My stomach dropped. My throat closed. My chest burned. My head throbbed. My anxiety took over. And I panicked.

She was describing *my* "treatments." These were *my* "manipulations."

If she was a victim, so was I.

Acceptance.

A rush of emotions raced through my body as I realized that I, too, was one of Larry Nassar's victims. The denial poured out of me and acceptance and anger took its place. I am incapable of writing the feelings that overwhelmed me in that moment. I'm not sure I could ever explain them well enough for another person to completely understand.

I felt myself cry, but I wasn't breathing heavily. The tears were just falling down my numb, cold cheeks. My phone stayed in front of my face, but I wasn't reading it anymore. I wasn't feeling any of my senses. I knew my chest was getting red from my anxiety, but it wasn't burning like it usually did. My phone was shaking in my hands, but I didn't feel myself trembling. My nerves shut down.

The first thing I did when my body finally started working again was reach out to one of my closest club gymnastics friends. I asked her what she was feeling, what she thought about the allegations, and if she had experienced the same "treatments" they were describing in the articles. She confirmed she was one of the anonymous victims to come forward. I thought, "Should I come forward too? Should I tell someone? . . . How do I tell my parents?"

I cried harder. This time my heart raced, and my breathing turned into an attack. How do I tell my parents? The people who spent their entire lives sacrificing everything they had to give me everything I needed, who gave their all to keep me safe. I imagined my mom crying, blaming herself for something she had absolutely no control over. My heart shattered into a million pieces imagining her hurt. I saw my dad becoming the person he was whenever someone hurt me or my sister. I saw him being dangerously aggressive in his pursuit for revenge for the way Larry had hurt me. I could feel his fury and imagined him brainstorming ways to get rid of the person who had assaulted his youngest daughter along with hundreds of other little girls.

I saw him reacting the way every father of every victim wanted to. "I won't tell them."

Instead, I connected with those I was closest to who offered the calmness I couldn't have found on my own. I was consoled by my roommates, my best friends, and my fiancé, Jake. They all comforted me and didn't ask questions. They weren't interested in the specifics; they were more concerned about me and how I was doing. They wanted to ensure that I was headed down a process of healing instead of down a darker path. I connected with more of the gymnasts I had been close to in club—more of Larry's victims.

I was surprised by the number of people who casually brought it up to me in conversation. Everyone knew I worked with Larry, and they were curious what my thoughts were. They had no problem asking, no sensitivity to my emotions, just curiosity about my involvement and connections.

"Have you seen the articles about your trainer, Larry?"

Duh.

The more victims who came forward, the more people asked. As the months went by and the case gained momentum from the victims coming forward, I became more anxious. As I was navigating the stages of acceptance, more allegations quickly surfaced. More stories and details came out, and I felt the acceptance process start over each and every time I read a new victim's account of the same "treatment" that I received from Larry.

I had to "accept" what Larry had done 350+ (reported) times.

Then new allegations began to unfold: child pornography. The world I had started to rebuild from the original allegations came crashing down again. Who was this man? Who was I seeing as my trainer? What kind of monster did I not recognize? How did I not see it?

I can't describe what it feels like when the person you trusted most as a child becomes such a demon on this earth. Trust is shattered. Sleep is impossible. Relationships seem unreal, fake. I hit a new low. My depression and high anxiety were back. I experienced seizurelike panic attacks over the smallest things. Changed plans? Panic attack. Difficult homework assignment? Panic attack. Burnt my frozen pizza? Panic attack.

It felt like everything I knew was a lie. My recent transition out of the sport had me feeling lost, and now I felt like the few things I was certain about weren't true. My trust in people was obliterated. My trust in humanity as a whole was demolished. And now? I have the great displeasure of feeling the effects of Larry's actions in all of my relationships.

My mind tricks me into believing that nobody is who they say they are.

Today, even the kindest actions feel dampened with ulterior motives. I thought Larry was the most selfless person on the planet for six years, and he turned out to be the greediest. I believe nobody. It is sickening. Someone makes me dinner, I think it's because they want me to give them something. Someone buys me flowers, I think it's because they're trying to make me do something. Nobody is nice anymore. There is no such thing as a genuine, selfless act.

My poor loved ones. Those who I mean something to have to push past this. They have to find a way to help me and tell me dozens of times that they need nothing in return. That flowers mean "I love you," and nothing more. That dinner ready for me when I come home from work means "I wanted to make your day easier," and nothing more. This is why I hate getting free drinks from strangers. I hate getting special treatment. I hate being approached in a specific way because some feel that if they are nice, they have a right to my personal space. No. Women do not deserve this. Nobody does. If the environment I am in is loud, you do not have a right to grab my lower back while leaning in toward my ear so I can hear you. If I sneeze, you do not have a right to touch my arm while saying, "Bless you." If I am leaving after a date you treated me to, you do not have a right to kiss me goodnight. Women don't need to be touched to know men are present. We owe men nothing for "chivalrous" acts.

I owed Larry nothing for letting him be my trainer, but he accepted rights to my body as payment for his "kindness."

Whatever confidence I had in my body was completely obliterated. On top of the disgustingly low confidence I had watching myself slowly adapt to the nonathletic body I grew into, I was now certain that my body had been abused for someone else's pleasure for six years. I felt like complete and total garbage. I felt dirty. My mind was living in the past, reliving the experiences. I took four showers a day for a long time. My skin always felt disgusting no matter how much soap I used.

My body had been used as a sex toy by a man thirty years older than I.

Because of Larry, I cringed when men gave me attention. I hated when men stared at me. I was struck with anxiety simply by being in the presence of men. I could not trust any of them. I would not trust any man. All of them were trying to use my body and doing whatever they had to do to build my trust to let them.

I was so angry at Larry.

~

CHAPTER FIFTEEN

Healing, Preparing, Recovery

My mind wasn't the only thing that required healing as 2017 began. Now that I was done with gymnastics, my body needed to finally be repaired too. I gave in to the doctors' suggestions from my sophomore year of high school and connected with a surgeon who had suggested a discectomy a few years back. (A discectomy is the surgical removal of of spinal discs that sit between the vertebrae.) Since my discs were bulging out into my spinal cord and killing the nerves that led to my legs, this seemed like the best procedure for me.

The surgeon I was going to see was located in Chicago—my parents trusted me only in the hands of the absolute best—and required a long drive out to see him. He requested I get an updated MRI to bring to my appointment. It had been a few years since I had gotten one, and I was interested to see if my back had changed at all. Larry had always told me my back was stable and wasn't continuing to bulge or cause more damage, so I figured it would look the same. I compiled all of my MRIs and presented them to him in June of 2017.

My parents and I met in Chicago with the mind-set that the discectomy would be happening that weekend. I had requested time off work and planned accordingly for the week's recovery the surgery required.

I hadn't predicted that Larry had lied about my prognosis.

My MRI images were clipped onto the screen. They looked horrendous. My back was not stable. The look on the doctors' faces was terror. The medical assistant who had taken the first look at the

MRIs ran them to the surgeon, who was headed into surgery with someone else.

She told me he asked how it was possible I walked into their office. She said I shouldn't have been able to walk at all. They told me the only option that I had: spinal fusion.

I wish I were making my story up. My life was falling apart at this point. Nothing was going right: I was in the middle of a drastic transition out of gymnastics, my trust in humanity was shattered—and apparently so was my spine. I felt like I was living in a soap opera. One domino after another fell in a continuous stream of trauma.

Spinal fusions are for sixty-year-olds at the youngest. My head wasn't absorbing what they were telling me. They wanted me in the next open surgery time. Everything was fuzzy. My mom and the nurse had their calendars out finding a date that would work. I was petrified. This surgery would be horrendous. It would be a nine-hour procedure with a full week spent in the hospital. A full year recovery. Half a year till I could even try running.

After the nurse left the room, my parents asked me if this is what I wanted.

The surgery absolutely terrified me. I thought it was a procedure I would get much later down the road and definitely after I had kids. I was scared. I was mad at Larry. I stared at my MRI. It looked so bad. I couldn't believe that was in my body. I swear at that moment it started to hurt as much as it should have years before. It was like when you dislocate your elbow and it doesn't hurt until you see it. I saw my injury and all of a sudden I was in excruciating pain.

I agreed to do the surgery.

It was scheduled just under a month after that appointment, and I would have to come back to Chicago on July 12 for surgery. Unlike most spinal fusions, instead of being at one level, mine would be at multiple. Four of my vertebrae needed to be fused together to make my back stable enough to function properly and not put my future ability to carry children, walk, and control my bladder in jeopardy. The surgery required the doctors to make incisions on my stomach and on my back. In total, it would be five new scars.

As if I didn't already hate my body enough, let's add some more imperfections to it.

I was more scared of the scars than I was of the recovery. I took extra long showers and ran my hands along my back and stomach, trying to make myself remember what it felt like to be scarless. I didn't want to forget, because I was about to be changed forever.

My loved ones did everything they could to make me feel better about the hell I was about to experience. Jake constantly told me how proud I should be of my scars, as they would be evidence of my strength and ability to push through massive amounts of pain. He reassured me that he thought I was beautiful, and that my scars wouldn't change that.

My parents connected with as many people as they could who had gone through the surgery already. They wanted me to ask them any questions that I had and reassure me that it was worth it. Everyone around me was trying to comfort me, but I was in my own world of terror. I felt like I was living in a nightmare. I walked around thinking my body had an expiration date.

I saw more effects of Larry's damage. My anxiety had begun manipulating my thoughts to imagine the worst-case scenario at all times. I had been so unprepared for the truth about Larry that I felt I had to prepare for the worst things at all times. I was trapped in my own head, constantly creating stories about or possible outcomes of my life.

A whirlwind of fear took over my head as I imagined everything that could go wrong with my surgery.

What if they damaged my spinal cord and I became paralyzed?

What if they nicked an organ in my abdomen and I died?

What if the anesthesia didn't work completely and I felt everything but couldn't say anything?

What if they gave me too much anesthesia and I died?

Nightmare upon nightmare. It was probably a good thing the surgery was planned so soon. As time went on, the scenarios I created in my head became more and more horrifying. I was a ball of panic as Jake and I drove to Chicago just under a month later.

My entire family met me in Chicago for my operation. We had a large hotel room that was hooked right onto the hospital, meant for the families of long-term patients. I would stay there with them the first night before I checked in for surgery at 6:00 the next morning.

We stayed up late playing games. I knew they were trying to distract me from the obvious terror I was feeling. They knew I didn't want to go to sleep. They knew I never wanted 6:00 a.m. to come. They were so good about doing everything they could to make sure I felt safe. My parents gave me a hospital kit filled with fun socks and loose-fitting clothes that would comfortably slide over my scars and swelling.

Everyone eventually had to go to bed; it would be a long day of waiting for them tomorrow. I looked out our bedroom window and saw a thunderstorm outside.

My final thought before I fell asleep was an anxiety-created scenario where the hospital lost power during my surgery and I didn't make it.

The morning of surgery I showered with the soap they gave me to use and threw my hair into a braid. I wasn't allowed to wear hairspray, perfume, makeup, or deodorant, so I looked like a gargoyle. My family and I walked over to the hospital and checked me in. I got all of the bands wrapped around my arm declaring me a patient, solidifying the reality of what was about to happen. They brought us to the waiting room where my family would stay for the next nine hours. The walls were covered with huge windows offering a stunning view of the city. The room was bright and warmly colored. I was in it for only five minutes before they called me back for operation prep.

I asked my mom and Jake to come back with me.

They handed me the surgical garments to put on, along with huge compression socks that went up to my knees. As I walked back to the bathroom to change, I saw the whiteboard with all of the surgeries happening that day. All were spinal fusions. I looked at the ages of the patients: 60. 62. 59. 71.

22.

I stood out like a sore thumb on the board. I was so young. I felt a wave of depression wash over me as I realized how broken I was at such a young age.

Thanks, gymnastics.

I changed into the clothes. I wasn't allowed to wear underwear or a bra. Usually this wouldn't be that traumatic, but everything with Larry made it worse. My mind-set when I was a kid had been that every doctor sees a thousand parts every day; they wouldn't remember my body.

That comfort didn't exist for me anymore.

I stayed in the bathroom for a while feeling massive amounts of discomfort in my vulnerability. I began thinking about how my naked body would be laid out under extremely bright lights for every doctor to see. This might actually have been my worst fear. I walked back to the preparation room and crawled into the bed. My mom and Jake sat beside me. There was a doctor on the other side of me running tests before surgery began.

"How will I go to the bathroom after surgery?" I asked. I couldn't sit in the silence anymore, so I decided to learn more about my procedure and its recovery.

"You'll have a catheter, you won't have to get up."

What???

My eyes shot straight to my mom. Nobody told me I would be getting a catheter, and she knew this added to my anxiety.

"You won't even feel it, and you'll be thankful you have it after surgery," the doctor said.

I had told Jake before coming to Chicago that I didn't want a catheter or a breathing tube because I was terrified of both of them. Nobody had told me I would have them before the surgery, so I thought I was safe. Now I knew I was getting one, so I had to ask about the other.

"I don't have a tube down my throat though, right?"

"We actually do have to put one in to protect your lungs. You'll be asleep when we put it in, and you won't remember when we take it out."

Oh my gosh. This could not be happening. This was a nightmare coming true. My eyes shot to Jake. He kept his face calm and unfazed for me, but he knew exactly what was going through my head.

"It's going to be okay, Rach," he said. "You won't feel it. It'll be okay."

My chest burned. My head was fuzzy. I was having a panic attack in front of everyone. Usually I can keep them private, but everyone was around me watching.

I never saw my surgeon on the day of my operation. I never got the chance to ask him why he didn't tell me about the catheter or the breathing tube. Before I knew it they had my hairnet on and both arms hooked up to IVs, and they were asking my mom and Jake to leave the room. My mom squeezed my foot gently as she walked out. My throat was closed, an explosion of tears wanted to burst out of my eyes. I was so terrified. I felt like I was saying goodbye. They wheeled me past my mom and Jake and started to administer the anesthesia. I heard my mom say, "I love you!" as they pushed me around the corner into the operating room.

The last thing I remember was seeing six huge, bright lights all aimed at the table in the middle of the room. Doctors in all blue with their faces covered were walking around, getting things ready. I saw so many machines.

I closed my eyes and thought, "Please, don't lose power."

I remember waking up. I was in a tiny space with curtains as walls. My eyes opened as a nurse began pulling the tube out from my throat. It felt like I was throwing up. It felt like I was gagging. The nurse was saying things to me, but I couldn't hear her.

I lay there for what felt like hours. I wiggled my toes. Not paralyzed. I analyzed my pain. It didn't hurt so much.

"Man, I'm tough," I thought.

I turned to face the nurse. I felt fine, and I wanted to see my family. I asked her if I could go see them. She told me I had to wait until my body had woken up a little bit more. In my head, I thought that if I kept talking to her she would think I was ready to go see them.

I would kill to watch a recording of what I was said; it was probably hysterical.

She wasn't letting me go even though I was talking her ear off, so I closed my eyes again. I heard my family come into my room, but my eyes wouldn't open. I heard my mom talking and the nurse telling them that everything went well. They said that they had trouble finding screws that were small enough for my spine, and that is why the surgery lasted longer than planned.

How long was it?

I opened my eyes. My mom, my dad, my sister, and Jake were all in the room.

I am not going to pretend I remember every detail about my time in the hospital. Conversations and specific details are extremely foggy because of the amount of medication I was on. I just remember how much pain I was in, what I had to go through to finally get discharged, and the terrible nightmare of the drive home.

My first night after surgery I tried desperately to find a comfortable position. Long story short, that position didn't exist. I had never been a back sleeper since it had hurt my back for the past six years to do so, so I demanded to sleep on my side. It took my parents, Jake, and the nurse on duty to turn me over and it was a lot of me yelling in pain to get there. They gave me a pillow to squeeze onto my belly since my new incision made it feel like my guts were falling out of my body. (That is no exaggeration of the pain.) They stuffed pillows behind my back because, believe it or not, you use your back muscles to sleep on your side. My back needed something to lean on so none of my muscles were engaged.

I was allowed to press my medication button every ten minutes to administer new doses of meds. It wouldn't light up any sooner than ten minutes, and when I saw that red light appear on my button I pushed no more than .2 seconds after. I could legitimately feel when ten minutes were up, as excruciating pain was creeping into my body. Only one person was allowed to stay with me in the room every night, and my mom always volunteered herself. There was no way I would've been able to sleep for longer than eight minutes if it weren't for my saint of a mother.

My first two nights in the hospital my mom set a vibrating alarm on her phone for every ten minutes, so she could press my medication button and I could sleep.

Just imagine that for a second, please. My mother, who had anxiously waited in a hospital waiting room for ten hours for me and who had exhausted herself my first day in the hospital taking care of me then sacrificed her own sleep so I wasn't in unbearable pain.

I twitched a lot in my sleep, which sucked. My muscles were battling the muscle relaxants trying to stay awake and therefore were twitching way more than normal. I felt like I was having seizures.

The second day in the hospital was horrendous. I still hadn't found food that I wanted to eat. Nothing sounded good. They were pumping me full of fluids so I was not necessarily hungry either. I managed to drink 3 percent of a cup of orange juice and take five bites of pudding.

Big mistake.

My stomach started to bloat. It pushed out through my brand-new incision on my belly and caused me massive amounts of pain in my stomach. Everytime I tried to eat, my belly got bigger. There was added pressure onto my back and belly because of the constipation. I hated eating, and so I refused to eat.

Just twenty-four hours after surgery, the nurse asked me to try standing up. I looked at her and thought there were horns in her head. This was a joke. I barely could roll onto my side and she was asking me to stand up? Absolutely not. But here she was, showing me how to best maneuver in order to stand. She started to lead my shoulders to the side to turn. I felt the pressure on my belly and back and squeezed my eyes shut to hold in the scream I wanted to let out.

"No no no no no," I said out loud.

I was done moving, I didn't want to move one more centimeter. I demanded to lie back down, but the nurse reminded me of the importance of standing for recovery. I wanted her to feel my pain so she understood how much I resented her at that moment.

She grabbed my legs and slowly moved them to dangle over the side of the bed. My family and Jake all got around me to help me stand. I wanted to cry. The pain was unbearable . . . and I had plenty of years' experience pushing through pain. This was a whole new level. I felt my guts tearing at my scar like they were going to come spilling out in one huge explosion. I felt my back's stiffness with every movement. My spine hurt. I can't explain what it feels like when your actual spine hurts. Usually it's just the muscles around it that cause pain, but my whole spine felt like it had been frozen solid for a hundred years and then forced to bend. It was so sore from having multiple screws forcefully drilled into it.

The nurse and my family lifted me to a standing position. I felt the blood rush from my face and I started to get tunnel vision. I felt the little bit of food I had consumed start to make its way back up into my throat.

I was going to throw up.

I had no stomach muscles; they had just been ripped apart, but they were about to convulse uncontrollably when I threw up. Terror took over my body. I honestly thought I was going to die. There was no way I was going to survive the pain of throwing up with freshly cut-open stomach muscles and a torn-apart spine.

I started having one of my seizurelike panic attacks.

Everyone helped lay me gently back down. My face was absolutely colorless as my mom handed me a trash can and scratched my upper back for comfort. I was bawling hysterically. I was so scared to throw up. My body was twitching and I was hyperventilating. My face began to tingle.

As I lay back down I felt my body begin to relax and the feeling that I was going to throw up slowly faded away. I started to calm down and my breathing slowed. The nurse asked me if I could feel my face, and my hands reached up to touch my cheeks.

Nope.

I lay flat and stared at my feet to try and calm down. The nurse said we would try to stand again in the afternoon. I'm pretty sure I gave her the meanest death glare I have ever given someone.

I can't lie: the doctor from my surgery preparations was right. I appreciated not having to get up to go to the bathroom. Trying to stand was the worst pain of my entire life. If I had to get up every time I had to go to the bathroom I probably would have just gone in my bed with no hesitation.

I was able to stand in the afternoon with the help of literally everyone in the room. Two people held my arms as I used them for balance, one person was behind me to catch me if I was going to keel over from throwing up, and one person dragged my IV machine next to me. I walked to the end of my room and back. Each step felt like someone was stabbing me in four places in my back and slicing me in half in my stomach. Every movement felt like death was about to take me.

Every day they weaned me more and more off the pain meds. They took my IVs and catheter out on the fourth day. I still had eaten almost nothing since surgery. I couldn't, because nothing was making its way through my digestive system. My system hadn't turned back on since surgery, and it wasn't allowing what I ate to make it to the other end. So everything I ate sat in my belly, growing and adding pressure to my scars. I was extremely constipated.

Trying to go to the bathroom after having my stomach ripped open was the worst experience. I imagine this is what women who have a cesarean birth experience go through during recovery. My mom would stand in the bathroom with me, wiping the sweat off my forehead and tears that were pouring out of my eyes as I sat in pain, unable to get rid of any of it. I had no stomach muscles to help me. I ended up needing multiple small procedures done to help get my system moving again.

Even though my dad and Jake ran to get every single little thing I wanted, held my hands and walked .0001 miles per hour with me around my hospital floor, and helped me move every time I needed to, I still hated my room. Even though my mom held my hand through every moment, helped me do things she hadn't had to help me with since I was a newborn, and stayed calm during every panic attack, I still resented my surgery.

My hospital stay was 100 percent traumatic.

Once my digestive system was finally able to turn back on, the hospital was allowed to discharge me. On the night of day six, they sat me in a wheelchair and quickly rolled me out of the hospital. I was slowly loaded into the front seat of the car to make the five-hour drive back to Minnesota while thinking that I was never going to be able to make it. I hadn't sat up in this position yet, and I was expected to stay in it for five straight hours.

During every single bump our car experienced, my back would get shot with a thousand needles. Every turn, brake, or acceleration I felt my shredded stomach muscles rip apart as they tried to engage.

We made it maybe fifteen miles before I felt the color leave my face and my stomach begin to convulse to throw up. We had to stop. I yelled at my mom to pull over.

We screeched into a gas station as Jake and my mom helped me out of the car and over to the grass to throw up. Standing actually felt better than the sitting position I had been in. I couldn't do the drive. I was not ready yet. My mom found a hotel a block away, and we checked in for the night.

Waking up the next morning I felt a hundred times better. I walked around the room (extremely slowly) and was able to eat a few Froot Loops. Jake and my mom brainstormed a new way to attack the long drive ahead. They layered pillows in the back seat to resemble a bed so I could lie flat instead of sitting and adding pressure to my incisions and screws.

This felt much better.

I had to use one hand to press onto the seats in front of me so if we braked my body wouldn't move forward, and the other hand to press on the seat I was on to prevent movement when we accelerated. I could do this. We stopped a few times so I could get up and walk around, and I walked a lot. We stopped at Panera Bread, and I was able to eat a few bites of my salad. I handled the drive so much better when I was lying down, and it put me in a much better mood.

Getting back to my apartment on campus was a relief. My bed had been lowered to the floor so I could just slowly fall onto it without having to climb or engage many muscles. I moved slowly for a few weeks, and my mom helped me with everything. She stayed in Minnesota with me for as long as I needed her. She helped me cook, she cleaned, and she sat outside the bathroom door for every shower.

She was also there when I took off my bandages and saw my scars for the first time.

No one had any idea what they would look like. Most of my family thought my stomach scar would run horizontally, because that is what the doctor had told them. I removed the back bandages first. I didn't care as much about what those looked like, and honestly, they weren't that bad. Four one-inch vertical incisions on the sides of my spine.

"Not terrible; I can live with these," I thought.

I slowly began to remove the large bandage over my stomach to reveal an enormous and gnarly vertical scar on my stomach. A six-inch scar ran from above my belly button to well below my bikini line on the left side of my body. I stared at it for a long time. It looked like the doctors had used patterned scrapbook scissors to cut me open. My belly was extremely swollen, so the scar looked like it was protruding forward even more.

I absolutely hated it.

No more two-piece swimsuits. No more crop tops. No way I would ever show my stomach ever again.

My mom was so comforting. She told me it wasn't bad at all, even though I knew it looked gruesome. She gave me a bunch of ideas about things to use to make it less prominent—oils, ointments, and lotions—and I got them all. She reminded me that the scars stood for so much more than just a surgery; they were also evidence of my resilience.

Week by week, I improved. When my mom left, she took my puppy with her since I was unable to take care of her by myself. My puppy yanked hard on her leash whenever she saw any animal outside, and it wrenched my back in ways that it shouldn't have. My family and I had also been planning a trip to Italy all year, and it was only a month after my hastily scheduled surgery. I wanted to get better quickly to get my puppy back and to be able to enjoy Italy as much as I could.

My spinal fusion experience was absolutely horrendous, but I am so happy that I did it. I am one year postoperation now. I can run with only soreness, not pain. I can lift any weight and not feel needles stabbing into my back. I can sleep on my belly, my back, and my side without a pillow. I can do cartwheels and feel absolutely no pain. I can go to the bathroom pain free. I can climb more than a flight of stairs without my legs getting too numb to move. I can stand and sit for longer than ten minutes. I can run my hands along my shins and feel it. I can lift my big toe and not let anyone push it down.

I would not have been able to get through that experience without my supportive sister, my selfless dad, my saint of a mother, and my chivalrous fiancé. They held my hand through it all and sacrificed everything to make sure that I was taken care of.

I thank God for them.

~

CHAPTER SIXTEEN

The Trial

A few months after my surgery, the storm of women fighting to take down the monstrous giant who had abused us for so many years plowed into trial. We were notified that we were allowed to give "victim statements," and more and more women latched onto the idea of being able to express their feelings of anger, resentment, and hatred toward the man who had caused them so much pain. More women were coming forward, accepting that they were victims, too.

Through months and months of denials, acceptance, pain, and the early stages of healing, I had accepted that I was a victim of Larry. I decided to do something about it. This past year, as his case came to trial and the victims were allowed to speak to him, I saw the ultimate opportunity.

I decided that I needed to speak, too.

Please know that this was no easy decision for me, or for any of the other survivors. There were so many hurdles I had to get over before I knew that this was what I needed to do. One hurdle was that I would publicly proclaim that I had been abused, that I was a victim. I would forever be tied to a treacherous and horrendous case. My body would forever be known as having been used by someone against my will. Another obstacle was that I had to see him. I had to stand in front of the monster, my demon, and tell him what he had done to me. Nobody can truly imagine the horror that accompanied just thinking of this.

But I wanted to take advantage of what was in front of me and gain closure with him. I reached out to my sister and told her what I wanted to do. She let me send her rough draft after rough draft, brainstorming what I would say. Looking back, I see how much my speech evolved. I can quite literally see the healing taking place through my words.

My first draft was so angry. I was yelling at Larry, screaming my pain at him. I was trying to throw my hurt at him with such force that maybe he would feel it, too. I told him how much I hated what he did to me, that no jail time would ever be long enough for what he did, and that his abuse would affect me for the rest of my life. I screamed, "How could you?" to him. I asked him, "Why?" I cried to him that I trusted him, that I had cared for him, how much he had meant to me. I watched myself pour my hurt into my words to try to use them as a way to cut him out.

And I watched woman after woman say exactly what I wrote in my first draft as they experienced the exact same feelings that I had.

But that first speech didn't make me feel better. In fact, it exhausted me. Every time I read my pain, I would sob. I relived my experiences through my words of hatred, and no healing was happening. This speech wasn't the closure my mind wanted, the ending my heart demanded. I reached out to my family for help in constructing something that would kickstart my healing, something that my mind and body could use to move past the horror that it was experiencing on a daily basis.

My parents had seen what was unfolding in front of them and were dealing with their own pain and acceptance. I cannot imagine what they went through, knowing their daughter had been abused for so many years by someone they trusted so much. This was the first time since the allegations were first released that I had talked openly and honestly about my true feelings toward my time with Larry as my trainer. This was the first time I actually admitted to my parents that he had abused me, but I know they had a concrete idea that I was one of his victims long before I confirmed it.

Honestly, telling my parents was harder than writing my speech to Larry.

I talked to my dad for a long time. He asked me questions about my feelings and about what I needed for my heart to be able to move on. He told me the story of his healing, and how he had originally reacted just the way that I predicted he would . . . the way that every father of every little girl reacts when he learns that a man has sexually molested his child. He told me about his journey to acceptance, to forgiveness. He asked me to turn to my faith for guidance, and so I did. He gave me Bible verses to look at for inspiration in writing my speech but reminded me that I needed to use *my* words and shouldn't be impacted by anyone else's. He told me that if I wanted to yell at Larry, I should yell; if I wanted to cry, I should cry. He told me that whatever I needed to say to start to heal, I should.

We then talked about my fear of facing Larry and speaking to him. My mind raced at the thought of him with that sulky, innocent face he had been presenting to the press for months. My body shuddered at the thought of just seeing his hands. His tools for abuse. I feared they remembered me, they remembered the feeling of my body. I went numb at the thought of his eyes looking at me, analyzing my figure, remembering how it felt on his bare hands. I imagined him picturing my "treatments" with him.

My chest burned red and blotchy.

My parents talked to me for a long time, telling me that whatever I needed or wanted to help my healing, they would be willing to do. They offered to fly me home, and my mom offered to drive ten hours from Michigan and travel back with me so I wasn't flying alone. She has always been so unbelievably selfless.

But my parents could sense my anxiety about just seeing Larry in person. After a long time brainstorming and asking questions about what I needed, my mom offered to read my statement for me. She volunteered to stand in front of the man who had abused her daughter, sometimes even in front of her, for years. She was willing to read my words and stand tall in front of a monster so that I would not have to. She volunteered to be my personal front line, my warrior, and fight the battle I was not yet strong enough to fight. As she always had done for me throughout my life, she threw herself forward as a sacrifice for me.

So I rewrote my statement. I spent hours writing things down, reading them out loud, and seeing if they made me feel more comforted with my abuse. I tested them to see if they would help me heal. I sent my final statement to my sister to read, and then sent it to the attorney representing us victims.

On January 23, 2018, both of my parents stood side by side in court in front of Larry Nassar.

As they approached the stand to face my demon and fight him together, they asked the cameras and microphones to be turned away from them to protect me. They refused to let something so horrible define me by being tied to me. I had been following the recording every day prior to this one, and as Victim 195 was given the floor to speak, the cameras turned to Larry and the sound was turned off. I knew my words were being read at that very moment.

I sat at my office at work, shut my eyes, and prayed.

Minutes felt like hours as I imagined my parents standing together, battling for me. I saw Larry's face with no sound. I saw his reaction to my words, but didn't know which words were impacting him. I saw his chin quiver and his eyes stare deeply at my parents. His gloomy, ashamed face stared at the faces of parents who had trusted their children with him. I watched his gaze never break as his presentation of innocence faded away into sadness and regret. I knew he was feeling what I was saying, I knew he was hurting. A monster who had lacked such empathy and emotion during previous statements was showing a sign of being human. After a few minutes, I saw his chin and eyes turn to face the floor, and the sound returned.

Minutes later, my mom called me. She told me it was over, that she had stayed strong and her voice never quavered. That she had tried her hardest to make each word I had said as powerful as she could. She explained that Larry had never looked away, and she felt that he had truly listened to my statement as it was different from the painful venting of the girls before me. Once my speech was over, we all swear we saw him turn to his defense attorney and mumble, "I can't do this anymore."

After this day, I can truly say my healing began. Knowing my parents had stood as one powerful force to fight for me created a foundation for rebuilding. Together, my parents and I ended my anger and hatred toward Larry Nassar. We ended my pain, embarrassment, and fear. They faced my demon, my monster, next to each other, and read him my impact statement, my closure.

Before this book, my statement was not released to the public. I was known only as Victim 195. The only people who heard my final words to Larry were those present in the courtroom that day.

Matthew 11:28: "Come to me all who are weary and burdened, and I will give you rest." My name is Rachel Haines, and I am a survivor of Larry Nassar.

Six years. For six years I came to you. I trusted you. My teammates trusted you. My parents trusted you. I was only thirteen years old. I was a child. And you took advantage of it. You ignored my character, my innocence, my age, my purity, and my rights.

Do you remember the injury that first brought me to you? It was a torn hamstring. Did that excite you? Did my injury make you happy because it meant you could do your "internal manipulation" on me?

Was my pain really your pleasure?

I always wondered why you volunteered to spend every Monday night at my gym. You donated hours to "fixing" us even though you had a family at home to take care of. You willingly stayed till eleven or midnight with no hesitation.

I gag at the thought of ever thinking of you as a saint for sacrificing time for us. It was not a volunteered sacrifice for you, it had a price we were unaware we were paying.

In 2011 I fractured my lower back. Did you remember my body from the hamstring injury? Do you know what it feels like to try and imagine what you were thinking about when you saw me? Are you even capable of empathizing with your victims?

How did you face my dad when working to construct a surgery for future backs like mine? As a father to daughters yourself, how could you do it?

I don't think you know this, but the consequences that so many other victims have stated that I too suffer because of your actions have a quickly approaching expiration date. Your sentence does not.

You always told me I was "the toughest kid you've ever met" because of the way I overcame obstacles. You frequently commented on my strength and my ability to push through excruciating pain. You have presented me my next obstacle I *will* overcome. Although I may not have had the strength to see you in person today . . . I am already on my way to forgiving you.

I've watched every video of the statements. I've seen your body language. I've watched you shake your head, cover your face with your hands, and cry. Your emotions remind me you are human. My faith reminds me you are a sinner . . . and all humans are sinners.

Larry, I forgive the human part of you. I will forgive the monster side of you soon enough, too.

I thought a lot about my statement. Whether or not I would even give a statement, what I would say, how I would say it, *who* would say it. I could have used this opportunity to admit all of the ways you have briefly weakened me.

But instead, I want to tell you how strong you have made me feel and how resilient I will be in the time to come. Your actions have brought together an unstoppable group of women, a relentless army. They have shown me a massive amount of support available to me. They have tested and strengthened my faith. They have challenged my morals. They have built up my character.

All of the effects of your actions are temporary. You may have taken advantage of my body, but my mind, faith, and spirit remain steadfast. I will spend my life getting stronger and you will continue answering for your actions even after you pass away. I hope that you pray for forgiveness, or I pray that you bring sunscreen to where you're headed.

I am tough. I am braver than your actions. I am stronger than your manipulations.

With this strength, I can say:

Larry, I forgive you.

"Blessed are the merciful. For they will be shown mercy." Matthew 5:7.

As Survivor 195, I can truly say that I have forgiven Larry Nassar. I have felt weight lifted from my shoulders as the anger and hatred that I was pouring toward him is gone. The energy I was using to fuel my fire of loathing against him has ceased.

I am now in a state of healing and recovery.

To My Fellow Sister Survivors,

From the absolute bottom of my heart, thank you. *Thank you for speaking loudly, for joining together, for standing tall. Thank you for not letting fear stand in your way. Thank you for fighting our monster, not just for yourself, but for all of us. Thank you for creating and being a part of our unstoppable army. Thank you for putting up with the victim shaming, the doubt, and the backlash. Thank you for continuing to fight even when it seemed everyone was against us. Thank you for knowing that what was done to us was unacceptable, and for not letting anything stop you from achieving justice.*

Now keep going.

Don't let anyone stop you on your pursuit. If anyone has ever made you feel uncomfortable or abused, keep fighting. Use your voice . . . and use it more. There will be shamers, doubters, and resistance. Remember what we fought for. Remember what we battled through. Remember how, together, we made the most powerful figure in the gymnastics community fall.

I am ashamed that we witnessed a system that required hundreds of voices to scream at them before they heard us. I am embarrassed to be a part of a society that didn't trust an accuser because her voice was of a higher pitch than the person she was accusing. We should not have needed a community, an army, to form before we brought one man to justice.

It is 2018. We are better than this.

Lastly, remember that we did not just come together to fight, we came together to heal. Now more than ever, we need to stand tall in union as we work past our horrifying experiences. Support each other as we navigate our recovery. Remind each other that we are not alone.

Remind each other that we are warriors.

CHAPTER SEVENTEEN

~

Still, I Rise

In the months to come, Larry's trial would unfold into something my emotions could not handle, and in some cases this was an amazing thing. In May 2018, I received the information that Michigan State had finally decided on a settlement amount for the survivors.

Five hundred million dollars.

Yes, this is an absolutely astronomical amount that I know we survivors are grateful to get. But, remember, this number is the price stamped on our abuse. Is there really a limit to what I am owed for six years of weekly abuse? Can you truly put a dollar amount on the discomfort, horrors, and other effects that I face because of the university's inability to take the actions it was supposed to? I personally think what Michigan State owes me for its failure to protect hundreds of women cannot amount to any price.

Within the same week of the settlement conclusion, I received an e-mail from ESPN about something that stretched far beyond my wildest dreams.

We sister survivors had won an ESPY.

We were invited to walk onto the stage in Los Angeles and accept the Arthur Ashe Courage Award. When I first read this e-mail I thought it was spam, a terrible joke. But when friend after friend, survivor after survivor, reached out to me in excitement and awe it finally hit. An award that had been previously won by prominent figures such as Muhammad Ali, William David Sanders, Nelson Mandela, and

Eunice Kennedy Shriver was being given to a group of women who spent years being trampled on and disregarded. ESPN was giving us the ultimate voice, the most powerful opportunity.

In the weeks to come, we received e-mail after e-mail from ESPN organizing and planning our experience to make it one of the most memorble ones of our lives. We were offered travel plans, lodging, hair and makeup, and more. I felt showered with compassion and the positive energy I needed.

ESPN made something positive out of something negative.

I personally felt honored and overjoyed at the opportunity ahead of me. My mind was a whirlwind of emotions. I connected with so many other girls to coordinate dresses, outfits, and plan get-togethers once we arrived in Los Angeles.

I cannot thank ESPN enough for the attention they gave us and the spotlight they shined on our movement. They built a platform on which we could stand tall and speak louder than we ever have before. They recognized that this type of courage was different and, unfortunately, not unique. They drew attention to the thousands of women who are abused, silenced, and ignored.

ESPN helped us shout, *"No more!"*

Epilogue

Originally, I debated writing my story. I feared being so vulnerable. I reflected on the person I was as a child and how I transitioned into who I am today. I watched my personality, beliefs, and motives evolve to match the demands of my sport. I forced myself to relive some of the moments I was trying to block out. I remembered my mistakes and instead of regretting them I thanked God for them.

I thank God for walking next to me through everything that he did. My past makes me the strong and invincible woman I am today. Gymnastics made me who I am today. I felt like I was stuck in the sport for so long. I was stuck in the dark culture. Even after I retired, my mind was still stuck in the sport. I still had to remain unique, still had to stand out at whatever I did.

I have to stand out at my job, with my friends, and with my family. I always have to find a way to win. Life is one big competition, after which I have to be on the top of the podium. I have to achieve a higher education than everyone, I have to earn more than everyone, I have to beat everyone in some way because winning is the only way I feel worth anything.

Gymnastics has equipped me with the skills to continuously win. I am competitive, motivated, and passionate about whatever I do. I have learned that my work ethic from gymnastics transitioned over into everything I do as an adult. I am an employee who accepts as many things that can fit onto my plate and gets them done—all thanks to the time-management skills I was forced to acquire as a Division I student-athlete. I continuously have among the highest weekly completed tasks numbers at my job because of the way gymnastics developed my competitiveness. Even my love language is "words of affirmation," because gymnastics is a constant routine in which people tell you how far away you are from perfection.

There is no denying that life has dealt me one crazy hand. I know my story as a gymnast was sometimes dark and depressing, but I am so thankful for every moment of it. I cried writing so many of these chapters. Some of them were tears of sadness, yes, but some of them were tears of joy in remembrance of the opportunities and experiences I had because I was a gymnast. I got to relive everything writing this book. I relived Nationals, committing to Minnesota, qualifying for the NCAA Championships, and doing a cartwheel for the first time pain free. I am so grateful to have been a gymnast, glad I went to Twistars, glad I went to Minnesota, glad I broke my back, and glad I worked with Larry Nassar.

Crazy, right?

Everything that happened to me shaped me into the person that I am today: this hard-working, unstoppable, unbreakable woman. Gymnastics did, in fact, give me those skills that every parent predicts it will give to their daughters when they enroll them in those Mommy and Me classes. I am coachable, goal oriented, respectful, and athletic. I can pick up just about any sport and be decent at it because I was a gymnast. I can apply to any job and know that no matter how much I may not know about it, I won't give up on being the best at it. I don't settle. If I set my mind to absolutely anything, it will get done.

Like the moment I said, "I am going to write a book."

Gymnastics did that to me.

Reflecting on my story has been an incredible journey—a journey I honestly have to thank Larry Nassar for. His case's storm blew a whole new level of strength into me. The creation of this army of women gave me a whole new perspective on resilience. The bravery his monstrous behavior instilled in hundreds of women made me feel like I had the voice I had never had before.

A voice I felt compelled to use.

I wrote my story to continue the healing I started when I wrote my statement to Larry. I wrote it to use as a beacon for change. I reflected on aspects of the sport that need to be updated. I wanted my story to inspire people to speak even more loudly about what they want to change. I wrote it to fuel the revolution forward.

This book was also my therapy. Something that started more as a journal ended as a book. It is my closure with the sport and, more importantly, closure with how it controlled me. Closure with how Larry used me. And it is the next step in my healing.

My life has been a constant stream of cue words: "Get up, get ready, drive to work, smile." I was living in a life that felt like a never-ending floor routine. For my entire life I have been trying to keep things as consistent as possible. I am so ready to close this chapter of my life. I wrote this book to put a period on the stream of cue words I have had in my head since I was a child.

I wrote this book to "stick it" one last time.

Current and Future Gymnasts,

I am two years out of gymnastics now. If I could go back and tell myself when I was a gymnast one thing, it would be to "embrace the moment." Time will absolutely fly. You will hear that a lot from everyone around you, too. But I don't just mean embrace the good moments, I mean embrace every moment. Hardships are going to happen. You are going to feel pain, both in your body and in your spirit. You are going to want to throw in the towel and quit . . . we all did at some point. You will get yelled at, discouraged, and probably also injured.

Embrace these moments.

These are the moments that shape you. Those hard and dark times are the times when the strongest fighters are built . . . when armies form. Those times when you can physically feel the weight on your shoulders and the pressure in your chest are the moments when you'll find strength you didn't know you had. You will leave gymnastics with mind and heart of the toughest warrior.

Embrace the moments when you feel the weakest—those times when nobody is standing behind you, nobody is holding your hand, nobody is believing in you. These are the moments when you learn to believe in yourself, because nobody can stop you once you have learned that. Let nobody stand in your way, let no doubt or fear survive in your thoughts. Nobody is in charge of your dreams but you.

~

About the Author

Michigan native **Rachel Haines** moved to Minnesota after high school to compete on the women's gymnastics team at the University of Minnesota. She competed for the team consistently for three years before retiring in 2016 due to injury. She was then a member of the gymnastics coaching staff as a graduate assistant until the completion of her master's degree in 2017.

At twenty-three years old, she holds a bachelor's degree in child psychology and a master of education in family social science. She is engaged to Jake Short, who was a wrestler at the University of Minnesota. Together, they have two dogs, Ellie and Odin.